Presented to

....

From

....

Date

....

365 Best-Loved

Bedtime Bible Stories

for Kids

ISBN 978-1-63609-267-6

Published by Barbour Publishing, Inc., 1810 Barbour Drive, Uhrichsville, Ohio 44683, www.barbourbooks.com.

Our mission is to inspire the world with the life-changing message of the Bible.

Printed in China.

001279 0722 XY

Jean Fischer

365 Best-Loved

Bedtime Bible Stories for Kids

BARBOUR kidz
A Division of Barbour Publishing

1

God Makes Everything! Part One

GENESIS 1:1–19

God has always been alive. In the beginning, He made the earth. The earth was empty, dark, and covered with water. Nothing lived there. Then God made night and day. He made the sky. He made dry land come out of the water and green plants grow. God made the sun, the moon, and the stars. He did all this in four days! And when God looked at what He had done, He saw that it was good.

2
God Makes Everything! Part Two

GENESIS 1:20–2:3

On day five, God filled the oceans with living things, and He made all the birds. On day six, God made every animal that lives on land. Then God did something even more amazing. He took dust from the earth, and He created a man! The man would be God's helper to rule over the animals and care for the earth. On day seven, God was pleased with everything He had done. His work was finished. So God blessed that day and made it holy—a special day to honor Him.

3
Adam Lives in the Garden
GENESIS 2:8–24

God named the man Adam. He made a big garden in Eden for Adam to live in. Four rivers ran through it. Beautiful plants and trees grew there, all of them filled with good food to eat. God put Adam in charge of the garden. He brought all the animals there and told Adam to give them names. Then God saw that Adam was alone. There were no other humans. "This is not good," God said. "I will make someone to be with Adam and to help him." So God created a woman.

4
Eve Is Tricked by the Snake
GENESIS 2:20–3:7

While Adam slept, God took a rib bone from his body. Then God, the Great Creator, turned the bone into a woman! Her name was Eve.

Adam and Eve cared for the garden. God let them eat food from every plant and tree except for one—the Tree of Knowing Good and Bad. "If you eat from that tree," God said, "you will die."

A sneaky snake wandered into the garden. He said to Eve, "Did God say you shouldn't eat fruit from this tree?"

"Yes," Eve said. "If we do, we will die."

"That's not true," the snake lied. "Eat it. You will be like God and know everything." So Eve ate the fruit. She gave some to Adam. Suddenly, they knew they had done a bad thing because they were afraid to be with God for the first time ever.

5

Adam and Eve Leave the Garden

GENESIS 3:8–24

When Adam and Eve heard God walking in the garden, they hid from Him.

"Where are you?" God called to them. "Did you eat from the tree I warned you about?"

"I was hiding from You because I was afraid," Adam answered. "Eve gave me the fruit. I ate it."

"The snake tricked me!" Eve said.

God said to the snake, "Because you did this, you will always crawl on your belly. You will hate the woman. She will hate you. And you and her children will fight."

Then God said, "Adam, you listened to Eve and ate from the tree. Now, for the rest of your life, you must work hard for everything you want. I made you from dust, so you will turn back into dust."

Then God sent them from the garden forever.

6
Cain and Abel
GENESIS 3:23–4:16

Adam and Eve had two boys, Cain and Abel. Cain was older. When they grew up, Cain worked as a farmer, and Abel was a shepherd. Both men brought gifts to God. Cain brought Him fruit. Abel brought a lamb. God was happy with the lamb but not the fruit. This made Cain very angry.

"Why are you so angry?" God asked him. "Be careful, because sin [everything bad in the world] wants to destroy you. It wants to rule over you."

But Cain didn't listen to God. When he thought God wasn't watching, Cain did a terrible thing. He allowed anger to rule over him. He killed his brother, Abel!

"What have you done?" God said. Then God punished Cain, and Cain ran away from God. He lived east of Eden in the land of Nod.

7
Noah Builds the Ark
GENESIS 6:1–7:5

Before long, the earth was filled with people. They were living in sin (letting everything bad in the world rule them). God saw there was one good man. His name was Noah. God said, "Noah, I'm going to start over. I'm sending a flood to cover the earth and destroy all I've created. You and your family are the only humans who will be saved. I want you to build a big boat, an ark. Bring two of every kind of animal into the ark and enough food to feed them and your family. When it rains, it will rain for forty days. Now go and do everything I have told you."

8
Noah Lives in the Ark
GENESIS 7:6–8:19

Noah did what God said. Then the rain started. It rained hard for forty days and forty nights. The ark floated safely on top of the water with Noah, his family, and the animals inside. After the rain stopped, the earth was flooded for almost half a year! When the water began to go down, Noah sent out a dove. The bird came back with an olive leaf, so Noah knew the earth was finally drying out.

One day, God said to Noah, "Bring your family and all the animals out." They came out of the ark and stepped, once again, onto dry land. They had lived in the ark for more than a year.

9
The Rainbow of God's Promise
GENESIS 8:20–9:17

The flood had ended. Every living thing on earth was gone except Noah, his family, and the animals on the ark. Noah built an altar—a special kind of table—where he placed gifts to honor God. He did this to thank God for saving his family.

"Never again will I allow a flood to destroy every living thing," God promised. "The four seasons will come and go forever. The earth is yours, Noah. Rule it well."

Then God did something special as a symbol of His promise to Noah. He placed a beautiful band of colors in the sky. It was the first rainbow ever! Every time you see a rainbow, you should remember God's promise to Noah.

10
God Appears to Abraham
GENESIS 12:1–13:18

Abraham was living in a city called Ur when God said to him, "Leave this place. Go to the land I will show you. I will make your family a great people. I will bless you and make your name great. Everyone on earth will be blessed because of you."

Abraham obeyed God. He and his family left their city, and God led them to a place called Canaan. Then God spoke to Abraham again. He said, "I will give this land to you and all your children." Abraham built an altar there to honor God and worship Him.

Lot, Abraham's nephew, had come with them to this new place. But Lot chose to live away from the others, in a valley near cities where people were not listening to God. Abraham stayed in Canaan, the land God had given him.

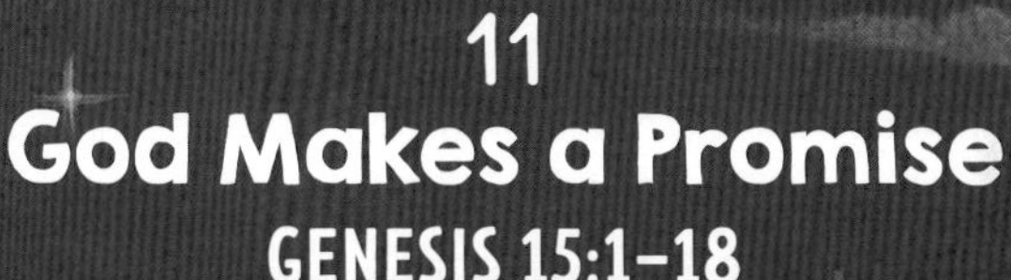

11
God Makes a Promise
GENESIS 15:1–18

One night, God came to Abraham in a special dream. “Don't be afraid, Abraham,” God said. “I will keep you safe and give you a great reward.” Then God took Abraham outside. “Look up. Try to count the stars. I promise you will have more children than there are stars. This land called Canaan will be theirs.”

Abraham was very old, and he had no children. Yet God said he would have more children than there are stars in the sky. Abraham trusted God and believed.

12
Sarah Laughs at God
GENESIS 18:1–15

One hot day, Abraham was sitting in the shade near his tent when nearby he saw God and two angels. They looked just like men! Abraham ran into the tent and told his wife, Sarah, to make lunch for their visitors.

"Where is your wife?" God asked Abraham. "She is going to have a child soon." In the tent, Sarah heard this and laughed. She was much too old to have children. "Why does she laugh?" God asked. "Nothing is too difficult for Me. At the right time, Sarah will have a baby."

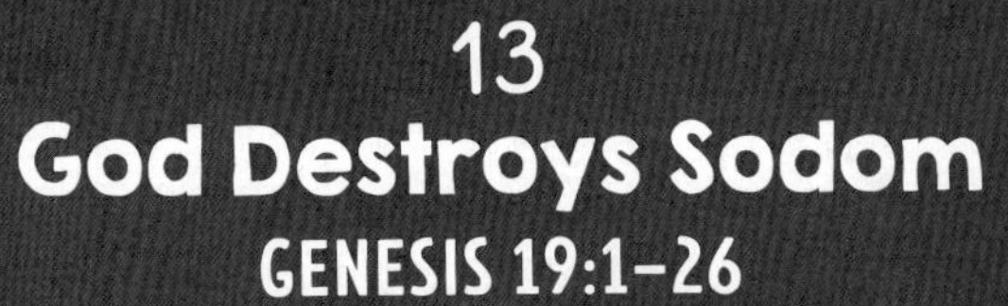

13
God Destroys Sodom
GENESIS 19:1–26

Abraham's nephew, Lot, lived with his family in a city called Sodom. It was an evil city, and God was so displeased with Sodom, He decided to destroy it. He sent His angels to warn Lot to leave. But Lot was in no hurry. The angels grabbed his hand and rushed him out with his wife and daughters. "Run for your life into the hills," the angels said. "Don't look back."

Fire came down on the city, and smoke covered the valley. Lot's wife disobeyed the angels. She looked back. And when she did, her body turned into salt.

14
Abraham's Two Sons
GENESIS 21:1–14

When Abraham was one hundred years old, God kept His promise. Sarah had a baby boy. They named him Isaac, which means "laughing," because Sarah had laughed at God.

Now Abraham had two little boys in his tent house: baby Isaac and Ishmael. Ishmael was the son of Sarah's maid. Ishmael treated Isaac badly, so Sarah told Abraham, "Send Ishmael and his mother away. I don't want Ishmael to have what belongs to Isaac."

This made Abraham sad because Ishmael was his son. But God said, "Abraham, don't worry. Do what Sarah says. It's better that Isaac lives alone with you and Sarah. Everything that is yours will belong to him someday. I'll take care of Ishmael. He'll be the father of a great family just like Isaac."

The next morning, Abraham told Ishmael and his mother to leave.

15
Ishmael's Desert Journey
GENESIS 21:14–20

Abraham gave Ishmael and his mother bread and water for their trip. But the water ran out. Ishmael's mother worried he might die in the hot desert sun. She sat him in the shade under a bush. Then Ishmael's mother cried. The angel of God heard and called to her from heaven. "Don't be afraid," the angel said. "Tell Ishmael to get up. Hold his hand. Ishmael will live and have a great family."

Suddenly, Ishmael's mother saw a well filled with water! There was plenty for them to drink.

God stayed with Ishmael through his whole life. Ishmael lived in the desert, and he became a great hunter.

16
Abraham Offers Isaac to God
GENESIS 22:1–19

"Abraham," God said, "I want you to take your son Isaac up on the mountain. I want you to give him to Me there as a gift." Usually, God asked Abraham to offer a lamb as a gift, never his son. But Abraham obeyed and went with Isaac up the mountain.

When they got there, Isaac asked his father, "Where is the lamb to give to God?" His father answered, "God will give us the lamb." Abraham loved Isaac. He didn't want to give him up. But Abraham always obeyed God.

Abraham was just about to let God take Isaac when an angel called to him, "Abraham, God knows you would do anything for Him—even give Him your son."

God was pleased with Abraham, and Abraham and Isaac went home together.

17

The Search for Isaac's Wife

GENESIS 24:1–27

When Isaac became a man, it was Abraham's job to find him a wife. Abraham wanted someone who worshipped God to marry Isaac. So Abraham sent his servant, Eliezer, back to his homeland to find a wife for Isaac. He knew the people there loved God.

Eliezer took ten camels and other precious gifts for the woman who would be just right for Isaac. Then Eliezer prayed, asking God to lead him to the one.

Soon Eliezer saw a beautiful young woman at a well. "Will you give me a drink?" he asked.

"I will!" said the woman. "I will give your camels a drink too."

The woman's name was Rebekah. She was one of many in Abraham's big family of aunts, uncles, and cousins. Rebekah invited Eliezer to come home with her and meet her family. Eliezer thanked God. He had found the perfect wife for Isaac.

18
Rebekah Marries Isaac
GENESIS 24:28–67

At Rebekah's house, Eliezer told Rebekah's family, "I am Abraham's servant. Your relative Abraham is a very rich man now, thanks to God. I promised to find a wife for his son Isaac. I asked God to lead me, and He led me to Rebekah."

Rebekah's father and brother agreed that she should marry Isaac. "God wants this to happen," they said.

Eliezer gave gifts to Rebekah and her family. They enjoyed a great feast together. Rebekah's father asked her, "Will you go with this man?" She answered, "I will go." Rebekah's family blessed her, and she left with Eliezer.

Isaac was walking in a field near his home when he saw Eliezer's camels coming with his bride. Rebekah also saw Isaac. It was love at first sight! Soon Isaac and Rebekah got married.

19
Esau Trades His Birthright
GENESIS 25:21–34

Rebekah and Isaac had twin boys. Esau was the first to be born. This meant he would get twice as much as his younger brother, Jacob, when their father died. The gifts Esau would get were called his "birthright."

When they grew to be men, Jacob was quiet, wise, and careful. He lived in a tent near his family. Esau was a hunter. His dad, Isaac, loved the tasty meat Esau brought home.

One day, Esau came home tired and hungry. His brother, Jacob, was making soup.

"Please give me some soup," Esau said.

"Will you trade it for your birthright?" Jacob asked.

"Why not?" answered Esau. "I'm about to die of hunger." So Esau promised Jacob his birthright.

Esau was foolish to trade his birthright for a bowl of soup. It meant he wouldn't get most of what their father owned.

20
Jacob Steals Esau's Blessing
GENESIS 27:1–38

In time, Isaac became very old. He knew he was about to die. So he said to his oldest son, Esau, "I want to bless you before I die. Hunt an animal and cook the meat for me. You know I love this. Then I will bless you."

Rebekah believed Jacob—not Esau—should get the blessing. So she cooked some meat and gave it to him. "Take this to your father. He doesn't see well, so pretend you are your brother, Esau. Then you will get the blessing."

Though it was wrong, Jacob stole Esau's blessing.

21
Jacob's Dream
GENESIS 27:41–28:19

After Jacob stole Esau's blessing, Esau was so angry he wanted to kill his brother! So Rebekah told her son Jacob to run away. "Hurry!" she said. "Go to your uncle Laban's house where you'll be safe." Jacob ran off carrying nothing but his walking stick.

At a place called Bethel, he was tired and lay down with his head resting on a stone. Jacob fell asleep. He dreamed he saw angels climbing a ladder up to heaven. Then God spoke to Jacob: "I am your father's God. This land is yours and your children's. The world will be blessed because of your family."

When Jacob woke up, he said, "This place is God's house. It is the gate of heaven."

22

Jacob Gets Married

GENESIS 29:1–30:24

Jacob found the same well where Eliezer had met his mother, Rebekah. A young woman was there giving her sheep a drink. She was Rachel, his uncle Laban's daughter. Right away, Jacob fell in love with her.

He promised Rachel's dad that he would work for him for seven years before he married Rachel. Jacob kept his promise. He loved Rachel so much. He couldn't wait to marry her. But on their wedding day, something happened. After they were called husband and wife, Jacob lifted his bride's veil, and instead of Rachel, it was her older sister! Rachel's dad had tricked him into marrying his oldest daughter.

Jacob had to work for Rachel's father seven more years before Jacob could marry Rachel. After they got married, they lived with Rachel's father and had many children. One of their sons was Joseph. Jacob loved him very much.

23
Jacob Travels Home
GENESIS 31:17–32:22

Jacob worked hard and became rich. Then, after many years, he decided to move home where he had lived with his parents and his brother, Esau. He packed up his big family and his huge herd of animals and left. This made Rachel's dad so angry that he and his men went after them. God said, "Don't harm Jacob." So instead, when they found Jacob, Rachel's dad blessed their family and went home.

Frightening news came to Jacob. His brother, Esau, was coming toward them with four hundred men! Jacob worried. He remembered stealing his brother's birthright and blessing. Would Esau still want to hurt him? Jacob divided his family into two groups for safety. Then he sent shepherds ahead with animals as gifts for Esau. Jacob stayed behind alone to pray.

24

God Wrestles with Jacob

GENESIS 32:24–32

While he was alone praying, Jacob felt someone grab him. It was night. Jacob couldn't see the man, but they wrestled almost until the sun came up. They wrestled until the man hurt Jacob's hip. Still, Jacob fought.

"Let me go," the man said.

"I won't let you go unless you pray that good will come to me," said Jacob.

The man asked, "What is your name?"

"Jacob."

"Not anymore," the man said. "From now on, your name will be Israel. You've wrestled with God and won."

Jacob wanted to know who this man was, but the man wouldn't tell him. The man would only bless him.

Jacob said, "I've seen God's face, and yet I'm still alive."

25
Joseph, the Dreamer
GENESIS 33:1-16; 35:16-19; 37:1-11

Jacob's brother, Esau, forgave him for stealing his birthright. He welcomed Jacob home. Jacob and Rachel had one more son. They named him Benjamin. And then, sadly, Rachel died.

Of all his sons, Jacob loved Joseph best. He gave Joseph a gift. It was a beautiful coat of many colors. Joseph's ten older brothers were jealous. They wished they could have a coat like his.

One day, Joseph said to his brothers, "Listen to the dreams I've had." Joseph told about a dream where his brothers' bundles of wheat bowed to him. In another dream the sun, moon, and eleven stars bowed to him.

When Joseph told them the dreams, his brothers knew their meaning: they would someday bow down to Joseph as their king. The brothers hated Joseph because of this.

26
The Dreamer Is Sold as a Slave
GENESIS 37:12–35

One day Jacob sent Joseph to check on his brothers who were caring for their sheep in the fields.

"Here comes the dreamer in his pretty coat!" said one brother.

"Let's throw him in the pit and say wild animals got him," said another.

So the brothers threw Joseph in the pit. They stole his coat and then sold him for twenty pieces of silver to slave owners who took him to Egypt. One brother, Reuben, went along with most of the plan, but he wasn't there when the brothers sold Joseph. He went back, deciding to rescue Joseph. But Joseph was already gone.

The brothers decided to lie to their dad about what they did. They stained Joseph's coat with animal blood and told Jacob that his son had been attacked by wild animals.

Jacob cried, "I will weep for my son the rest of my life."

27
Joseph, the Slave
GENESIS 39:1–40:22

Joseph was bought by Potiphar, a leader in Egypt's army. God was always with Joseph. Potiphar liked Joseph. He trusted Joseph and put him in charge of taking care of Potiphar's house.

One day, Potiphar's wife wanted Joseph to do something bad, but he said no. Then the woman told her husband an evil lie about Joseph, and Potiphar locked Joseph in prison. The prison guard liked Joseph. He gave him important work to do.

The butler and baker to Egypt's king were also prisoners. The men had strange dreams, and when they told Joseph, he said, "Maybe God will tell me the meaning of your dreams." And God did! He told Joseph that the butler would be set free. "When that happens," Joseph told the butler, "tell the king to give me my freedom." God's news for the baker wasn't good. The baker was in big trouble for his crime.

28
Pharaoh Sends for Joseph
GENESIS 40:23–41:16

The butler was freed from prison. But it was two years before he remembered Joseph.

"I'm dreaming strange dreams," Egypt's king, Pharaoh, told the butler. "No one can tell me what they mean."

Then the butler remembered. "Joseph! The man locked in your prison. He told me what my dreams meant—and he was right."

Pharaoh sent for Joseph, and soon, Joseph stood before him. "I've heard that you tell the meaning of dreams," said Pharaoh.

"I don't know the meaning," Joseph replied. "But God does. He will give you the answer."

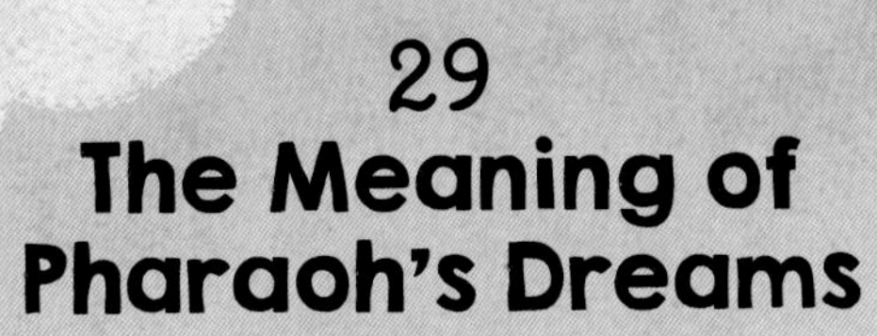

29

The Meaning of Pharaoh's Dreams

GENESIS 41:17–36

"In my dream, I saw seven fat cows eating grass by the river," Pharaoh said. "Then seven skinny cows came. They ate the fat cows. But they were just as skinny as before. In another dream, I saw seven good heads of grain on one stalk. Another stalk grew next to that one. It had seven poor heads of grain. The poor heads of grain swallowed the good ones. But they stayed poor."

"God is showing you what He will do in Egypt," Joseph said. "Seven years of very good crops will come. Then there will be seven years with no food. You need a wise man to help Egypt." Joseph continued, "He must save some of the good crops so people will have something to eat when there are no crops. Then your people won't starve."

30
Pharaoh Honors Joseph
GENESIS 41:37–45

Pharaoh asked his servants, "Can we find anyone like this young man? The spirit of God is in him." Then he said to Joseph, "God has shown you all this. There is no one wiser than you. You shall be in charge of my palace and my country. I'm greater than you only because I'm king."

Then Pharaoh gave his own ring to Joseph, and Joseph was given the best clothes. A gold chain was placed around his neck. Joseph rode in his own chariot. And wherever he went, the people bowed to him.

31
Joseph's Brothers Visit Him Part One
GENESIS 41:46–42:7

Joseph got married and had two sons. When the crops were good, he was careful to save plenty of food. Then seven years came with no food. All the people in the land were hungry. They went to Pharaoh, asking for something to eat. "Go to Joseph," he said. Then Joseph sold food to the people. Soon, the whole world asked Joseph for food.

Joseph's father and brothers needed food too. All the brothers, except Benjamin, traveled from their home in Canaan to Egypt to ask for help. When they saw Joseph and bowed to him, they didn't know he was their brother. Joseph looked much older than he did years ago when they had sold him to be a slave. But Joseph knew who they were.

32
Joseph's Brothers Visit Him Part Two

GENESIS 42:6–24

The brothers bowed to Joseph again, still not knowing who he was. They thought that he was just a man Pharaoh put in charge.

"Who are you?" Joseph asked, although he knew who they were. "Are you spies?"

"No, sir. We are brothers," they said. "The youngest is at home."

"You must prove you aren't spies," said Joseph. "One of you must stay here. The others may leave with your family's food. Bring your youngest brother back to me. Then I'll know you're not spies."

Joseph made one brother, Simeon, stay. Joseph wouldn't let him go until the other brothers returned with Benjamin.

As the brothers left, Joseph heard them say, "This bad thing is happening to us because years ago we sold our brother as a slave."

When Joseph heard this, he cried. He knew his brothers were sorry for what they had done.

33
Joseph's Brothers Return Home
GENESIS 42:25–43:15

When the brothers arrived back home, they discovered that Joseph had given them the food for free. Their money was in the bags with the food.

When they told their father that they had left Simeon in Egypt, Jacob cried. "First my son Joseph died, and now Simeon is gone. And you want to take Benjamin from me. If I lose Benjamin, I'll die. It was a mistake that the money was in your bags. Take special gifts back with you and twice as much as you owe. May God have mercy on you!"

So Jacob's sons took Benjamin and returned to Egypt. Soon they were bowing down to Joseph again.

34
Joseph's Brothers Visit Him Part Three
GENESIS 43:16–44:13

Joseph saw his brothers coming with Benjamin. "Bring them to my house for a feast," he told the servants.

The brothers were afraid to see Joseph. They said to the servants, "We brought back the money that was in the bags."

"God gave you the money," a servant said. Then he brought Simeon out, and Joseph came into the room. All the brothers bowed.

Joseph asked, "Is your father well?"

They answered, "Our father is well." Joseph looked with love at his little brother, Benjamin. He was so happy to see him that he cried.

They ate a big feast together. But the brothers still didn't know Joseph's secret. When they left with more food, Joseph hid his special silver cup in Benjamin's bag. He did this to make them return one more time.

35
Happy Brothers
GENESIS 44:14–45:16

When the brothers returned with the silver cup, Joseph looked at Benjamin and said, "The one who stole it will stay here and be my slave."

Another brother, Judah, spoke up. "Benjamin's father is old. His son Joseph was already killed by wild animals. He'll die if his son Benjamin doesn't return. Take me as your slave instead. Then the boy can go back to his father."

Joseph couldn't keep his secret any longer. He cried out, "I'm Joseph, your brother! You sold me as a slave and lied about me being dead. But God made something good come of it. Look! I've given food to all the world."

Then Joseph hugged Benjamin and cried. The brothers all hugged, and they made up. Everyone was happy again.

36
Joseph's Family Moves to Egypt
GENESIS 45:25–47:10

Pharaoh was pleased that Joseph and his brothers were together again. He said, "Tell your family to move here." So Joseph sent his brothers home with money, new clothes, and donkeys loaded with grain and bread.

The brothers ran to Jacob and said, "Father! Joseph is alive." They explained what had happened.

"I must go see him," Jacob said.

On the way, Jacob worshipped God. God said to him, "Don't be afraid to go to Egypt. I'll go with you. Your family will become a great nation."

More than seventy people in Jacob's family moved to Egypt.

When Jacob finally saw his son Joseph, he said, "Now that I know you're alive, I can die in peace."

Pharaoh asked Jacob, "How old are you?"

Jacob answered, "I am 130 years old." And he blessed Pharaoh.

37
Joseph Dies
GENESIS 47:27–50:26

God gave Jacob a new name—Israel. Israel lived in Egypt near Joseph. He was almost 150 years old when he died. His sons buried Israel back in his homeland, Canaan, near his father, Isaac, and grandfather, Abraham.

Joseph's brothers still worried he might be angry with them for selling him as a slave. "Please forgive us," they said.

"What you did was bad," Joseph told them. "But God used it for good. Look at all the children in Israel's family. Don't worry. I'll always provide for you."

Joseph lived 110 years. Before he died, he said to his brothers, "One day, God will tell you to go home to Canaan. When you do, take my bones back with you." So, after he died, Joseph's bones were kept in a stone coffin. The brothers knew that one day they would carry him back to his homeland.

38
A Mean New King
EXODUS 1:6–22

Years passed, and Israel's people filled the land. The Egyptians had a new king. He didn't remember Joseph. This pharaoh worried that the Israelites would become more powerful than he was. So he made Israel's people into slaves. They worked hard for Pharaoh, and he was mean to them. But still, they continued to grow in number.

Then Pharaoh made a terrible new rule. All the baby boys born to the Israelites had to be thrown into the river.

39
Moses
EXODUS 2:1–10

One mother decided to hide her baby boy from Pharaoh. She hid him for three months. Then, when she worried she couldn't hide him any longer, she wove a basket. She made it so no water could leak in. Then she put her baby boy inside and floated the basket among the reeds by the river.

Pharaoh's daughter enjoyed bathing at that place on the river. She found the floating basket and felt sorry for the crying baby. She decided to keep him, and she named him Moses.

40
A Stranger in a Strange Land
EXODUS 2:11–25

Moses grew up in Pharaoh's palace in Egypt. He became a wise and powerful prince. Still, he loved his own people, the Israelites. They were Pharaoh's slaves, and when Moses tried to help them, it made Pharaoh very angry. So Moses ran away.

Moses met a pretty, young girl, and they got married. They lived in her father's house, and Moses took care of his sheep. For many years, Moses had lived a good life in Egypt. Now he lived in a desert caring for sheep. "I'm a stranger living in a strange land," Moses said.

Meanwhile, the Israelites suffered as Pharaoh's slaves. God saw them. He remembered His promises to Abraham, Isaac, and Jacob. And He knew He would help them.

41
Moses and the Burning Bush
EXODUS 3:1–6

One day, Moses was in the mountains taking care of his sheep. At Mount Horeb, God appeared to him as a flame of fire in a bush. Moses was amazed that the bush wasn't burning up!

God called from the bush, "Moses, Moses."

"I'm here," Moses answered.

"Come no closer," God warned. "Take off your sandals. You're standing on holy ground. I am the God of your ancestors—the God of Abraham, of Isaac, and of Jacob."

Moses felt afraid. He hid his face and couldn't look at God.

42
Moses Is Sent to Egypt
EXODUS 3:7–4:31

“I've seen the Israelites suffering,” God told Moses. “I plan to set them free from Egypt and send them to a land flowing with milk and honey. I'm sending you to tell Pharaoh to let My people go. Say, ‘I AM sent me to you.’ Tell them the God of Abraham, of Isaac, and of Jacob has sent you.”

“But I'm nobody!” Moses said. “What if they don't believe me?”

“Throw down your shepherd's staff,” God said. Moses threw it down, and it became a snake! “Do what I've said,” God told him. “I will show you other signs and wonders. Take your brother, Aaron, along to help you.”

Moses and Aaron bowed to God and worshipped Him. They went to tell Pharaoh to let God's people go.

43
Moses Speaks to Pharaoh
EXODUS 5:1–7:13

Moses and Aaron went to Pharaoh. "This is God speaking to you," they said. "Let My people go so they can serve Me."

This made Pharaoh even angrier and meaner to the Israelites.

Moses went away and prayed. "God, why did You send me to Pharaoh?"

God told him, "Go back to Pharaoh. Show him the sign I gave you." So Moses and Aaron returned. Aaron threw down his staff. It became a snake. Then Pharaoh's magicians did the same thing. But Aaron's staff swallowed up their snakes in one big gulp.

44
Blood and Frogs in Egypt
EXODUS 7:14–8:15

God told Moses, "Pharaoh's heart is hard toward Me. Go to the Nile River with your staff. Tell Pharaoh, 'God says, "Let My people go!"' Then hit the water with your staff. It will turn to blood."

Moses did what God said. The river turned to blood. It smelled bad, and all the fish died. Still Pharaoh's heart stayed hard. He wouldn't let God's people go.

Moses and Aaron went to Pharaoh again and said, "God says, 'Let My people go!' " Aaron held his staff over the river. Frogs came up and covered Egypt. There were so many frogs, they even got into people's beds and ovens.

"Tell God to make the frogs go away, and I'll free His people," Pharaoh promised. God made all the frogs die. They were piled up in heaps and smelled terrible. But Pharaoh hardened his heart again. He didn't let God's people go.

45
Terrible Days in Egypt
EXODUS 8:16–10:29

Pharaoh wouldn't let God's people go. So Aaron hit the ground with his staff. A cloud of dust turned into fleas that bit all the people. But Pharaoh didn't care. A swarm of flies filled Egypt. Still Pharaoh's heart was hard toward God. A terrible disease killed all Egypt's horses, cattle, and sheep. People got sores all over their bodies. Hail fell and killed the crops, and grasshoppers ate what was left over. Still Pharaoh's heart was hard.

"I never want to see you again," Pharaoh said to Moses.

"It's true," Moses replied. "You'll never see me again."

46
God's Passover
EXODUS 12:1–30

God told Moses, "In a few days, you are to leave Egypt. I want all the Israelites to find a perfect lamb. On the fourteenth day of the month, they must give it to Me as a gift. Put its blood on every doorframe. I am going to do something terrible to Egypt, but when I see blood on the door, I will pass over that house. This is My 'Passover.' You will always remember this day."

The Israelites did what God said. Night came, and a great cry went up all over Egypt. Every house had trouble. But God passed over the Israelites' houses that had blood on their doors.

47
The Exodus
EXODUS 12:30–14:14

Every house had trouble, even Pharaoh's. "Take God's people, and get away from here," he told Moses. The Israelites had been Egypt's slaves for 430 years. But that night, they all walked away with Moses ahead of them—the Bible calls this "the exodus."

God was their leader. In the daytime, God appeared in a tall cloud. At night, He appeared in a column of fire. The Israelites traveled all the way to the Red Sea. But, back in Egypt, Pharaoh was sorry he'd let them go. He sent his army of soldiers on horses and in chariots after them.

The Israelites were trapped with the sea in front of them and mountains on each side.

48
Escape through the Sea
EXODUS 14:13–30

The Israelites cried out to Moses for help. "The Lord will fight for you!" he said. Then Moses lifted his staff up toward the Red Sea. "You will never see the Egyptians again!"

An east wind blew. The water in the Red Sea split in half, and its floor became dry. The Israelites walked on this path to the other side of the sea with a wall of water on both sides of them.

The Egyptians were close behind. But before they could enter the path through the sea, Moses lifted his staff again. The walls of water tumbled down, swallowing up Pharaoh's army.

49

A Song of Thanks

EXODUS 15:1–25

Safe on the other side of the Red Sea, Moses wrote a song of thanks to God. The Israelites sang:

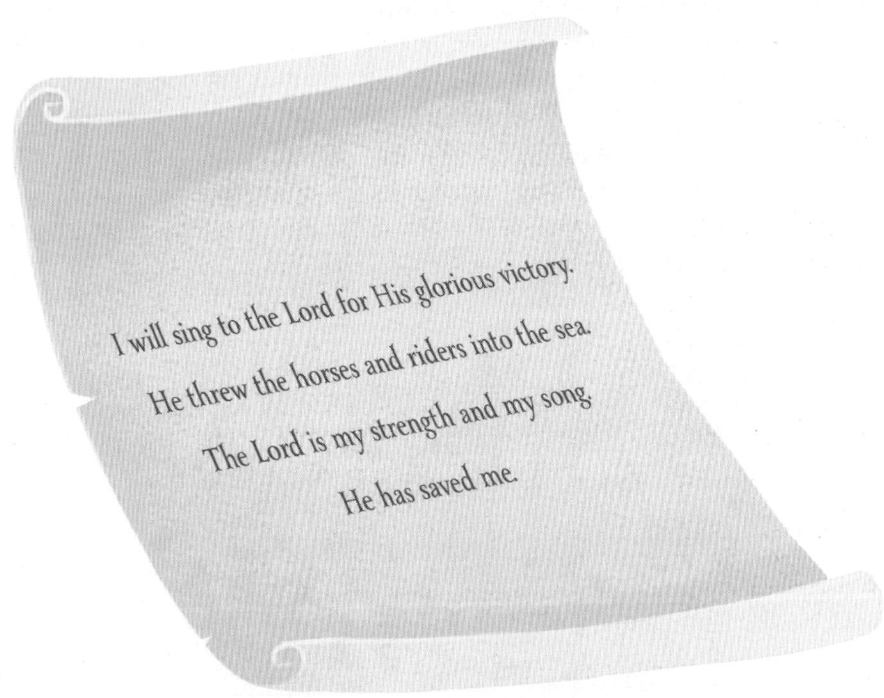

As they traveled through a huge desert, the Israelites were thirsty. They found a pool of water, but it tasted bad. God told Moses, "Cut a small tree and throw it into the water." Moses did what God said, and this made the water fresh.

50
Food Rains from Heaven
EXODUS 15:27–16:35

The Israelites came to a place with twelve freshwater springs. But they had no food. They were starving and wished they had stayed in Egypt.

God said to Moses, "I'm going to rain food from heaven for My people. Every day they'll go out and gather enough for that day."

The next morning, little white flakes like frost fell to the ground. "What is it?" the people asked. "This is the bread God has given you," Moses answered. "Gather what you need. Don't keep any leftovers. They'll spoil." Every morning they gathered as much as they needed. But when the sun got hot, the food melted on the ground. Some tried to keep it overnight, but it became stinky and filled with worms. The Israelites called this food "manna," which means "What is it?" As they traveled through the desert, they ate manna every day for the next forty years!

51
Water Comes from a Rock
EXODUS 17:1–7

As the Israelites continued to travel through the desert to the land God had promised them, water was hard to find. They became angry with their leader, Moses. "Did you bring us from Egypt so we would die? Find us some water!" they cried.

Moses prayed, "God, what should I do?"

"Bring the staff you used to part the Red Sea," God said. "I'll be standing on a rock at the place called Horeb. Hit the rock with your staff, and water will flow out."

Moses did this, and the Israelites had plenty to drink.

52
Moses, God, and the Mountain
EXODUS 19:1–24:18

The Israelites camped at a place called Mount Sinai. God was there in this holy place. The people went to the mountain to meet Him. The mountain was wrapped in thick smoke, and God was there in a fire. The mountain shook, and the sound of a loud trumpet blasted through the smoke. Moses spoke to God, and He answered in thunder. When the people saw God's amazing power, they were afraid.

God called Moses to the mountaintop. He stayed there with God for forty days. God gave Moses two stone tablets. On them God wrote ten special rules He wants people to follow. They are called the Ten Commandments.

53
The People Worship a Golden Calf
EXODUS 32:1–6

Moses had been on the mountaintop for weeks, and the people were worried because he hadn't come down. They lost faith in God. Still, they wanted to bow down and honor *something*. So they made their own god—a calf made of gold.

Moses' brother, Aaron, built an altar to worship it. "This is your god, O Israel!" the people shouted. "It saved you out of Egypt."

The next morning, they had a big party. The people ate and drank and danced all day. They had turned away from God and began doing wicked things that He did not like.

54
Moses Smashes the Golden Calf
EXODUS 32:7–34:4

"Go down the mountain to your people," God told Moses. "They have made a false god—an idol—that they worship. I'm very angry with them!"

"O Lord," Moses prayed, "I will go there and make things right."

When Moses saw the wild party, he was so angry that he threw down the stone tablets, and they broke. Then he took the statue of the gold calf off the altar. He smashed it, burned it, and ground it to dust.

"Who is on the real God's side?" he asked. Then Moses went back up the mountain with two new stone tablets.

55
Moses' Face Shines Brightly
EXODUS 34:5–35

Again, Moses spent forty days on the mountaintop with God. The Lord talked with Moses, and then He wrote His Ten Commandments again on the new stone tablets.

When Moses brought the tablets down the mountainside, his face lit up with God's light. Moses' face shone so brightly that it was hard for the Israelites to look at him without the light blinding their eyes.

After Moses spoke to them about God's commandments, he covered his face with a veil. The bright light surrounding his face hurt everyone's eyes when they looked at him.

56
God's Tabernacle
EXODUS 35:1–40:38

God showed Moses how to build a meeting tent, a place where the Israelites could meet with Him. It would be called "God's tabernacle."

The people used their very best materials when building it: gold, fine cloth and leather, spices and oils, wood and precious stones. Inside, the walls were covered in gold, and there was beautiful furniture. The tent was made of blue, scarlet, and purple cloth, and outside was a brass altar for offerings to God.

The tent could be packed up and carried with the Israelites when they traveled. It was exactly as God had planned it, and His Spirit filled it with His glory.

57

Inside the Tabernacle

EXODUS 35:1–40:38

The tent was big—forty-five feet long, fifteen feet wide, and fifteen feet high. It had two rooms. One was called "the Holy Place." The other was called "the Holy of Holies."

In the Holy Place were three things: a gold table with twelve loaves of bread; a gold lampstand with seven lamps; and an altar for incense. The Holy of Holies was God's special place. Only the high priest was allowed in that room. It held a perfect gold box called "the ark of the covenant." Inside the box were the two stone tablets with God's Ten Commandments.

58
Tabernacle Priests
EXODUS 28:1–5

God decided that Moses' brother, Aaron, and Aaron's sons would be priests. They would lead the people in worship and care for the tabernacle.

The high priest wore a beautiful robe and hat. On his chest was a covering of precious stones. Only priests could go into the meeting tent. The priests never wore shoes inside. They filled the lamps with oil so they were always burning, and they kept fresh bread in the tent and burned incense to honor God.

Some of the Israelite men served as helpers to Aaron and his sons.

59

Two Goats

LEVITICUS 16:7–10

Once a year came the Day of Atonement—a special day when people asked God to forgive their sins. Two of the best goats were chosen. One goat was given to God as an offering—a giving of their best in exchange for God forgiving the people's sins. The high priest placed his hands on the second goat's head. Then he listed sins that needed to be forgiven. The second goat was released into the wilderness forever. This was a symbol of the people's sins being taken away.

60
Spies
NUMBERS 13:1–33

The Israelites packed up the meeting tent—the tabernacle—and followed God. Finally, they arrived just outside Canaan, the land God had promised them.

Moses sent twelve spies to check out the new land. People lived there who did not belong—it was the Israelites' land, a gift from God.

When the spies returned, they carried huge bunches of grapes. "This land flows with milk and honey," they said—meaning it had plenty to eat and drink. "But the people are strong and the cities like forts. The men are so big we felt like little grasshoppers."

The people were afraid when they heard this. They forgot that God always keeps His promises. He had promised to give them Canaan. But still, the people were afraid to enter their land.

61

The Israelites Wander in the Desert

NUMBERS 14:1–45

The Israelites grumbled and complained. "Let's go back to Egypt," they said. This made God angry.

"How long will you mistrust and disobey Me?" God said. "Tomorrow you must go back to the desert. You will wander there for forty years."

Then the people changed their minds. "No," they said. "We won't go back to the desert. We'll go straight into the land right now."

Moses warned them, "Don't. God will not be with you." But they went anyway. And the armies that lived on the land attacked them. Finally, they obeyed God and went back to the desert.

They wandered in the desert for forty years, and the men were trained to fight the enemy armies when they returned to the Promised Land.

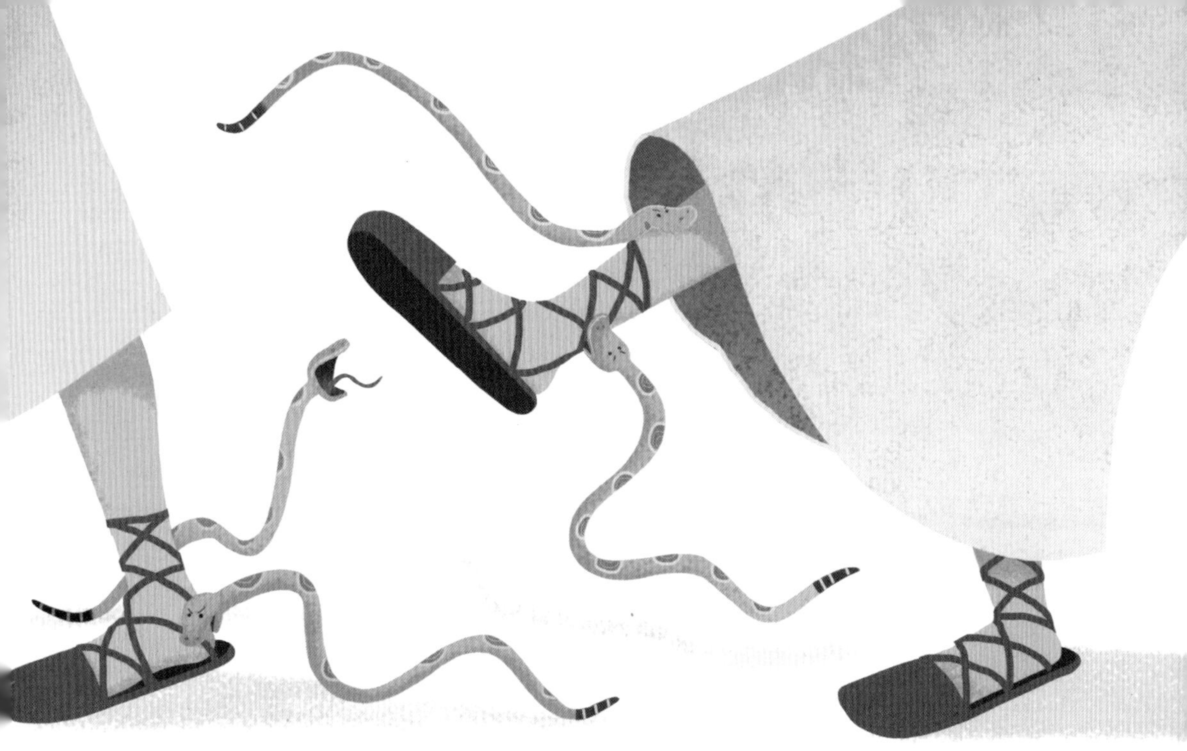

62
A Bronze Snake
NUMBERS 21:5–9

As they wandered in the desert, the Israelites kept complaining to God and Moses. "Why did you bring us from Egypt to die?" they moaned. "We have no water, and we're sick of eating manna."

God became even angrier. He didn't stop poisonous snakes from entering the Israelites' camp and biting the people. Some people died from their snakebites.

"We've sinned," the people told their leader, Moses. "God is angry."

So God told Moses to make a snake out of bronze. "Hang it on a pole," God said. "Whoever looks at it will not die."

Moses did this. People bitten by the snakes looked at the bronze serpent and lived.

63

Moses Dies

DEUTERONOMY 34:1–12

When Moses was 120 years old, he left the Israelites' camp alone. He slowly climbed to a mountaintop, where God spoke to him. "This is the land I promised to Abraham, Isaac, and Jacob. You can look at it from here, but you can't go in," God said.

Moses died while he was on the mountaintop, and God buried him there. There was never again anyone like Moses.

64
A Man Named Job
JOB 1:1–2:6

Job lived near the Promised Land. He was a rich man and very good.

One day, angels stood at God's heavenly throne. Satan was there too. "Have you seen Job?" God asked. "There's no one like him. He never does anything wrong."

"Take away everything he has, and he will turn away from You," Satan said.

So God decided to show Satan just how faithful Job was. He said, "Do what you want with him." Then Satan brought Job trouble. He took away most of Job's family, his animals—almost *everything*!

Job said, "I came into this world with nothing. I'll leave with nothing. The Lord gave me everything; He can take it away."

God said to Satan, "Have you seen Job? He's blameless and right."

"Give me power to make him sick," Satan said. "Then we'll see how good he is."

So God told Satan, "Do what you want."

65

Job Stays Faithful to God

JOB 2:7–42:17

Satan caused painful sores to form all over Job's body. But Job stayed faithful to God. He would not blame God.

Job's wife blamed God, though. "You should be angry with God!" she told her husband.

"We take the good along with the bad," Job told her.

Job's friends thought he must have done something so evil that God was punishing him. But Job knew this wasn't true. He was good, and he believed in God's goodness.

Then God spoke to Job's friends. "You don't speak the truth about Me, but Job does," God said.

Job prayed for his friends. God made Satan stop causing Job trouble. Then God gave Job twice as much as he'd lost.

66
Joshua, Jericho, and the Jordan River
JOSHUA 1:1–2:1

After Moses died, God chose Joshua to lead the Israelites. "Lead them across the Jordan River," God told Joshua. "I will give them the land I promised them. Be strong and brave. I will be with you, just as I was with Moses."

Joshua led the Israelites to camp on the riverbank. The river was almost overflowing. Only a strong man could swim across, and they had no boats. Across the river, the people could see the strong walls of Jericho. Before they could take the land God had promised, they had to take this city.

Joshua chose two brave and wise men as spies. "Go find out all you can about Jericho and the land beyond." The men swam across the river and entered Jericho. They spent the night in the house of a woman named Rahab.

67
The Woman with the Scarlet Rope
JOSHUA 2:2–24

When Jericho's king learned there were spies at Rahab's house, he sent soldiers to arrest them. Rahab hurried to hide the men. Then she told the soldiers, "Yes, the men came to me. But I didn't know where they were from. When it was time for the gate to be shut after dark, they left. I don't know where they went. Be quick! Go after them, and you will catch them."

Before the spies went to bed that night, Rahab said to them, "I know God has given you this land. Promise me that your army won't hurt my family."

The spies answered, "We promise, because you've saved our lives." Rahab let down a scarlet rope for them to escape. "Our army will see this red rope hanging out your window," the spies told her. "It will be a sign for them not to harm your family."

68
The Israelites Cross the River
JOSHUA 3:1–17

The spies reported to Joshua about their trip to Jericho. Then Joshua told the Israelites it was time to cross the river. The priests led the way, carrying the ark of the covenant. The river water rushed along, swift and strong. God told Joshua, "Have the priests stand in the river. I will cut off the rushing water, making it safe to cross." So the priests walked into the river, and the water stood still. Just like when they crossed the Red Sea, the river water piled up in a heap. The Israelites crossed the river on a dry path down its middle. When they were safely on the other side, the river filled up and began to rush again.

69

Jericho's Wall Falls Down

JOSHUA 6:1–27

"The city of Jericho belongs to your people," God told Joshua. Then He told Joshua what He wanted the Israelites to do.

Their army marched toward the city, ready to fight. The priests carried the ark of the covenant and held trumpets made of rams' horns. God said that for six days they should march around the city's wall just once while blowing their trumpets. On the seventh day, God said to march around seven times while sounding their trumpets. That day, after one long blast of a ram's horn, all the Israelites shouted, and the wall around Jericho fell! Then the Israelite army went in and took the city that belonged to them.

70
The Gibeonites Lie
JOSHUA 9:1–27

A tribe of people called the Gibeonites lived on the land that belonged to the Israelites. They decided to make peace. The men of Gibeon came to Joshua wearing worn and ragged clothes. "We live far away on your land. The things you did at Jericho are well known," they said. "We want to be your friends."

Joshua and the Israelites made peace with the Gibeonites. But then they learned the Gibeonites had lied about where they lived. Their camp wasn't far away. It was very close.

"Why did you lie?" Joshua asked.

"We heard God promised you this land," they answered. "We were afraid for our lives. Now you can do what you want with us."

Joshua made them woodcutters and water carriers for Israel. From that time on, the people of Gibeon served the camp of Israel.

71
The Fight for the Promised Land
JOSHUA 10:1–11:23

Jerusalem was the largest city on the Israelites' land. Its people worshipped idols instead of the real God. When Jerusalem's king heard the Gibeonites had made peace with the Israelites, he planned to destroy them.

The Gibeonites said to Joshua, "Come quickly and help us. Hurry, before it's too late. The whole country is coming to harm us."

Joshua called out his army. Then a great battle began. God helped by raining hailstones on the Israelites' enemies. The Israelites destroyed the armies of five kings. Then Joshua turned north to fight the kings there. It took many years and many battles before the Israelites finally took back all the land God had promised them.

72
Joshua Divides the Land
JOSHUA 15:1–19:51

God told Joshua to divide the land among His people. There were twelve tribes of Israelites, one tribe for each of Jacob's sons. Two and a half tribes already had their land on the other side of the Jordan River. Nine and a half tribes still needed to be given their land.

Judah was given land in the mountains near the Dead Sea. Simeon's land was near the desert. Benjamin's was north of Judah's. In the middle was Ephraim's land. Joshua lived there. The rest of Jacob's ancestors were given their parts, and then this big country, made up of the land God had promised them, became known as the land of Israel.

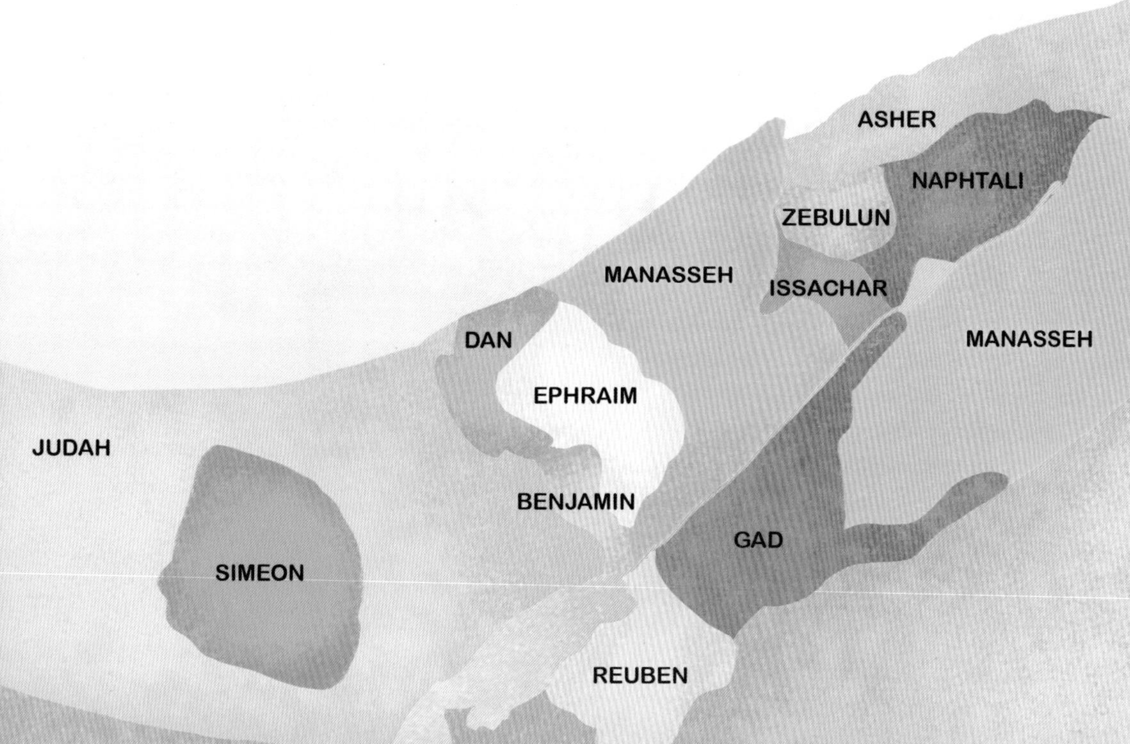

73
Israel's Safe Cities
JOSHUA 20:1–9

God had told Moses that there should be six cities in the land of Israel that would always be safe if someone innocent was accused of a crime. Sometimes accidents happened and no one was at fault. But sometimes people were falsely blamed for making an accident happen, and they were in danger of being hurt by angry people. So God demanded that there be safe cities where the innocent people could go and live. This, and other rules God made, helped the Israelites to live safer and better lives.

74
The Altar by the River
JOSHUA 22:1–34

Most of the Israelite tribes worshipped God at a tabernacle Joshua had set up in a place called Shiloh. It was near the center of Israel, and it was the only place God allowed them to worship.

The tribes who lived on the other side of the Jordan River set up their own altar. This upset the people worshipping in Shiloh. Two places to worship meant that Israel was divided. God didn't want this. The tribes almost went to war with each other.

"Why do you have that new altar?" the tribes at Shiloh asked.

The tribes east of the Jordan River answered, "Our altar isn't for worship. It is there to remind our children that Israel is one people on two sides of a river. It's to remind them that God is the Lord of us all."

75
Joshua's Last Days
JOSHUA 23:1–24:33

When Joshua was more than one hundred years old, he called the leaders of the twelve tribes to come to him. He told them the story of the Israelites, beginning with God telling Abraham that his ancestors would become a great nation. Joshua reminded them of all the good things God had done. Then, knowing he was old and might die soon, Joshua gave this advice: "Respect and honor God. Serve Him with all your heart."

The leaders promised, "We will."

Joshua set a huge stone by an oak tree as a symbol of the leaders' promise. Ten years later, Joshua died. The Israelites served God for as long as they remembered Joshua.

76

Israel Forgets God

JUDGES 1:1–3:7

After a while, the Israelites forgot about all the good things God had done. They stopped obeying Him. They hadn't chased away others living on their land, and they had begun to worship things that were not the real, true God.

This made God angry, so He allowed trouble in their lives. Enemies attacked them and robbed them. Their grain, grapes, olive oil, and animals were gone.

When things got bad, they would cry to God for help. God sent wise judges to make good decisions. He wanted the Israelites to turn to Him and be saved. Sometimes it worked. They would turn to God and serve Him. But then they would slip back into their old ways and displease Him. This happened many times.

77
Judge Deborah
JUDGES 4:1–7

A woman named Deborah became one of Israel's judges. She was the only woman judge. Deborah held court in the hills of Ephraim. She sat under a palm tree, giving advice and solving problems. Deborah had God's Spirit with her. This is why people trusted her and followed her advice.

One day war broke out when the army of a king named Jabin attacked the Israelites. Deborah knew what God wanted the people to do. She sent for a military commander named Barak. "God commands you to gather an army," she said. "He will lead you to defeat the king's army."

78
Two Women Help to Save Israel
JUDGES 4:8–24

Barak said to Deborah, "I won't go to war unless you go with me."

"I will go with you," she said. "But you haven't always trusted God, so you won't get the honor when we win. God will give this victory to a woman."

Ten thousand men joined them in the fight, but their army was small compared to the king's. The Israelites fought anyway. The king's army was not ready, so the Israelites took them by surprise. The king's soldiers ran away. God helped the Israelites by making a river flood its banks. The king's general escaped to the home of a woman named Jael and spent the night there. She tricked him into thinking she would help him, but instead she stopped him from leading his troops—forever.

Thanks to the bravery of Deborah and Jael, Israel was saved!

79
Gideon Meets God
JUDGES 6:1–32

The Israelites continued to turn away from God, and trouble came. An army, the Midianites, raided their land. The Israelites ran away and hid in caves. They cried out to God for help.

A man named Gideon was cutting wheat when he saw an angel. The angel said, "You are a mighty warrior, Gideon. The Lord is with you. Go and save Israel from the Midianites."

Gideon's family wasn't powerful, and he was the youngest in his family. "How can I save Israel?" he asked.

God spoke to Gideon: "I will be with you." Gideon brought an offering for God. He put it on a rock. Fire came and burned up the offering, and then God disappeared.

That night, Gideon and ten men destroyed the Israelites' statue of Baal, their false god. Then Gideon built an altar and made another offering to the one true God.

80
Gideon's Fleece
JUDGES 6:33–7:1

God was with Gideon. A cry went out to Israel, "Come help us drive out the Midianites." Israel's soldiers came to help Gideon. But the Midianite army was powerful and strong.

Gideon wondered if he was doing what God wanted. "God," Gideon prayed, "I'm going to lay a fleece of wool on the floor where grain is harvested. Give me this sign: tomorrow, dew will be on the fleece but not on the ground. Then I'll know we'll defeat the Midianites." The next morning, the fleece was dripping with dew. The ground around it was dry. Gideon said, "God, give me one more sign. Tomorrow morning, make the fleece dry and the ground wet with dew. Then I'll have no doubt." The next morning, the ground was wet and the fleece was dry. So Gideon and his troops prepared for war.

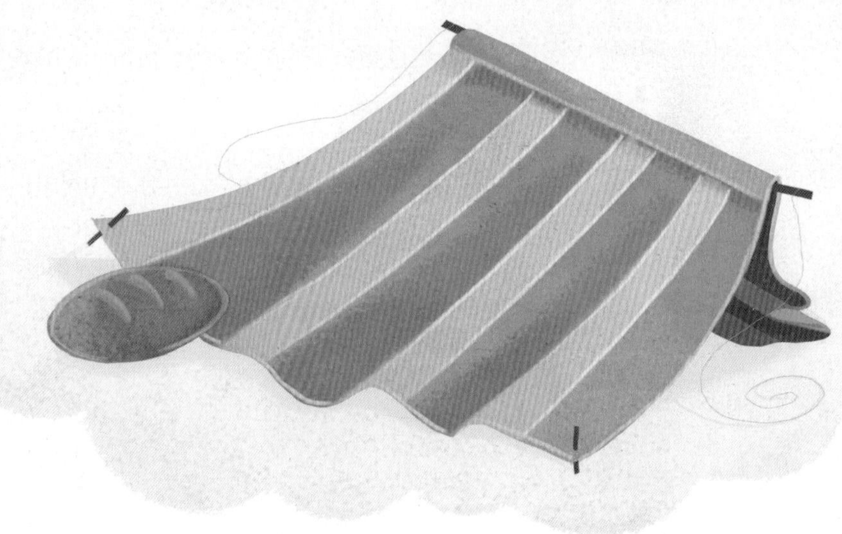

81
Gideon's Tiny Army
JUDGES 7:2–15

God said, "Gideon, your army is too big. People will say the Israelites won because their soldiers were powerful. Send home everyone who is afraid."

Twenty-two thousand men went away. Ten thousand stayed to fight.

Then God said, "Send the ten thousand to drink at the spring. Send home those who kneel and lap up water with their tongues. Keep those who scoop up water and drink from their hands."

Only three hundred soldiers were left!

God told Gideon to go in the night and spy on the Midianites and listen to what they said. Gideon heard a soldier say, "I dreamed a loaf of bread tumbled into our camp. It hit the tent and knocked it down." Another soldier said, "Maybe it's a sign that Gideon's army will defeat us."

Gideon was glad the Midianites were afraid. He thanked God and prepared for battle.

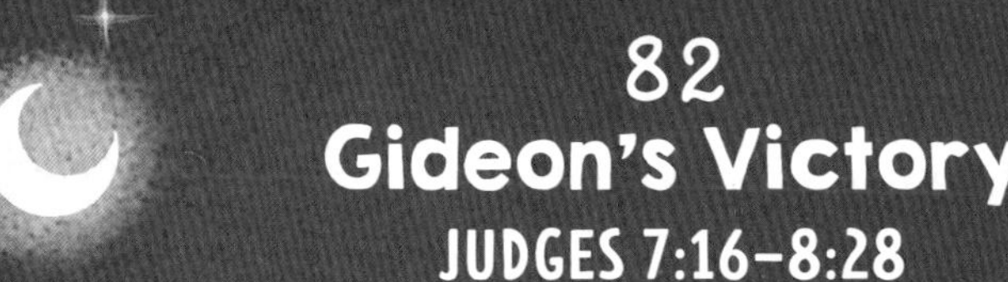

82
Gideon's Victory
JUDGES 7:16–8:28

Gideon divided his army into three parts, one hundred men in each. Every soldier held a trumpet and a clay jar with a lamp hidden inside. Silently, they moved in the night. At the edge of the Midianites' camp, they blew their trumpets. Then came the sound of their clay jars breaking. The lamps flashed their light. The Israelites shouted, "The sword of the Lord and of Gideon!" The Midianites began to run. Confused, they started to fight each other! The tribes of Israel chased the Midianites away, and the Midianites never attacked Israel again. God's tiny army had won!

For forty years, Gideon served as a judge in Israel. For as long as he served, there was peace. The people wanted to make him king, but Gideon said, "No, the Lord God is the King of Israel. Only God will rule these tribes."

83
Jephthah's Foolish Promise
JUDGES 11:1–40

After Gideon died, Israel went back to forgetting God. They began to worship idols again. So God gave them over to their enemies. One day, an enemy army, the Ammonites, attacked Israel. This time, a man named Jephthah was God's helper to set the Israelites free. But before he led the soldiers in battle, Jephthah made a foolish promise. He said, "God, give me victory. Then I will give to You whoever greets me first when I get home."

With Jephthah leading the Israelites, God allowed them to win the war. When Jephthah got home, the first one to greet him was his little daughter. He didn't want to give her to God, but he had made a promise. His daughter stayed with Jephthah two months before she went to be with God.

84
Samson, the Strongman
JUDGES 13:1–14:4

Among Israel's enemies were the Philistines. They took all the Israelites' swords and spears so they couldn't fight. Then they robbed Israel of their crops so they would starve. The people cried to God, and God heard them.

God sent an angel to the wife of a man named Manoah. The angel said, "You will have a son. When he grows up, he will save Israel from the Philistines. Your son must never drink any wine. His hair must never be cut. One day, he will be a priest and help Israel take away the Philistines' power."

The woman named her baby Samson. When he grew up, his body was big, powerful, and strong.

When Samson decided to marry a Philistine woman, his parents were unhappy. But they didn't know God would use this marriage. It would help free Israel from the Philistines.

85

The Honey-Filled Lion

JUDGES 14:5–9

Soon before his wedding, Samson was walking through a vineyard—a place where grapes grow. Suddenly, a huge lion appeared. It roared at Samson, ready to attack. But God's Spirit was with Samson. With all his power and strength, Samson grabbed that lion and tore it apart. Then he went on his way. He didn't tell anyone what had happened.

Later, as he walked to his wedding, Samson stopped to see if the dead lion was still there. He found its body filled with bees and honey. Samson scooped up some honey and ate it. He gave some of the sweet treat to his parents, but he didn't tell them where he had found it.

86
The Riddle at the Wedding
JUDGES 14:10–20

At Samson's wedding celebration, the Philistines told riddles. "I have one," said Samson. "If you answer it, I'll give you thirty suits of clothes. If not, you give me thirty."

They agreed. "Tell us your riddle."

Samson said, "Out of the eater came something to eat. Out of the strong came something sweet." The Philistines didn't know the answer. So they went to Samson's wife. "Find out the answer, or we'll burn your house down!"

She went to Samson. "If you love me, tell me the answer." Samson didn't want to, but finally he told her about the lion and the honey. Then she told the Philistines how to answer the riddle. Samson lost the game. He had to give them thirty suits. He was so angry he fought the Philistines and took their clothes. Then he left his wife and went home to his parents' house.

87
A Jawbone Kills a Thousand
JUDGES 15:9–16:5

A tribe of Philistines attacked one of the tribes of Israel. "What do you want from us?" the Israelites asked.

"We want Samson," they answered.

So three thousand Israelites went to see Samson. "You've done harm to the Philistines," they said. "We're suffering because of what you did." Then they tied Samson up and took him to the Philistines. When they saw Samson brought to them in ropes, the Philistines cheered. But then Samson did something unexpected. He broke through the ropes as if they were string. He grabbed a dead mule's jawbone, and with it, he fought the Philistines until none were left.

In time, Samson fell in love with a Philistine woman named Delilah. The Philistine rulers came to her and said, "Find out what makes Samson so strong. If you help us, we'll give you 1,100 pieces of silver."

88
The Strongman's Secret
JUDGES 16:6–15

Delilah asked Samson three times what made him so strong. Three times he lied. He said if he were tied up with seven new bowstrings or new ropes that had never been used, he would lose his strength, or he would become weak if someone braided his hair. "You must work the seven strings of my hair into the cloth you are making on your loom and hold it there with a nail. Then I will become weak and be like any other man," he said. So while Samson slept, Delilah wove his hair. But, when Samson woke up, he used all his strength to break her loom.

"How can you tell me you love me when you've lied to me?" Delilah cried.

89
Samson's Strength Is Lost
JUDGES 16:16–22

Day after day, Delilah begged Samson for the secret of his strength. Finally, he told her, "My hair has never been cut. When I was born, God made me a priest. If my hair is cut, then my vow with Him will be broken. My great strength will leave me." (Remember: an angel told Samson's mother that he should never cut his hair.)

That night, while Samson slept with his head on Delilah's lap, Delilah let the Philistines come inside, and they cut off his hair.

"Wake up, Samson!" Delilah cried. "The Philistines are here!"

Samson jumped up thinking he had all the strength to fight off his enemies. But his strength was gone. The Philistines hurt Samson so badly that he could no longer see. Then they took him and locked him up in their prison.

In time, Samson's hair began to grow long again.

90

Samson Dies

JUDGES 16:23–31

The Philistines praised their false god, Dagon, for allowing them to capture Samson. Three thousand Philistines gathered in the false god's temple to celebrate. "Bring in Samson to entertain us," they said and laughed.

Samson came out, and they made fun of him. They made him stand between the tall stone pillars that held up the building. Samson said, "Let me rest against the pillars." Then Samson prayed, "God, remember me and strengthen me. Let me pay the Philistines back for what they have done to me." Samson leaned against the pillars, pushing with all his might, and the building fell. The Philistines died, and so did Samson. But finally, he had defeated his enemies.

91
Naomi and Ruth
RUTH 1:1–22

A woman named Naomi had a husband and two sons. The sons married two beautiful women. But one day, Naomi's husband and her sons died. Now Naomi and her sons' wives were alone.

Naomi decided to move to Bethlehem in Israel. She told her sons' wives, "Return to where you grew up. May God be kind to you there." She kissed them both, and they cried.

One of the women did go back to her homeland. But the other, Ruth, wouldn't leave Naomi. "Don't make me leave you," Ruth said. "Where you go, I'll go. Where you live, I'll live. Your people will be my people, and your God, my God. Where you die, I'll die, and there I'll be buried. Only death will come between us."

Naomi said, "No. You should return to your family."

But Ruth refused. So she and Naomi went together to Bethlehem.

92
Ruth Meets Boaz
RUTH 2:1–9

It was barley harvesting time in Bethlehem. When the Israelites harvested their fields, they always left some behind for poor people to glean, which means "to gather up."

Ruth said to Naomi, "Let me go to the field to gather grain." So Ruth went to glean in the fields owned by a man named Boaz.

Boaz was watching the harvest and saw Ruth. "Who is the young woman gleaning in my field?" he asked his workers.

"She came back here with Naomi," they answered.

Boaz invited Ruth to stay in his field and glean. "I have told the servants not to bother you," he said. "When you are thirsty, go to the water jars. Drink the water the servants have put there."

93

Ruth, the Mother of Kings

RUTH 2:10–4:22

"I've heard you came here with Naomi," Boaz told Ruth. "The Lord sent you. May He reward you." Boaz gave Ruth food for her lunch and spoke to the harvesters. "Be kind to her. Leave plenty of grain."

That night Ruth showed Naomi all her gleanings. She told Naomi of the kind, rich man. "He is a relative of my dead husband," Naomi told her. "Stay in his field until the harvest ends."

Boaz held a great feast at the harvest's end. At the celebration, Naomi told Ruth to go talk with Boaz. "Please be kind to me," Ruth said to him, "because my husband was Naomi's son, and Naomi's husband was your relative."

Boaz was more than kind to Ruth. He married her! Ruth and Boaz had children, and their great-grandson was David, who became the king of Israel.

94
Samuel Stays in God's House
1 SAMUEL 1:1–2:21

A priest named Eli and his grown sons served God in the tabernacle. A man named Elkanah and his family worshipped there. The man's wife, Hannah, cried because she had no children. She stood outside the tabernacle praying, "O Lord, look how sad I am. Allow me to have a little boy. I will give him back to serve You."

God heard Hannah's prayer and gave her a baby boy. She named him Samuel, which means "asked of God." When Samuel was still a little child, Hannah brought him to the priest, Eli. Hannah said to him, "I asked God for this boy. I promised him to the Lord for all his life. Let him stay here with you and grow up in God's house."

So little Samuel stayed at the tabernacle, helping Eli, who was getting old. Samuel was like a son to him.

95
God Calls Samuel
1 SAMUEL 3:1–10

Little Samuel lay resting in the tabernacle when he heard someone call his name. "Samuel, Samuel."

"Here I am!" said Samuel, running to Eli's room. "Did you call me?"

"No," Eli answered. "Go back to bed, my son."

The same thing happened a second time and a third. Samuel didn't know who was calling his name, so he kept running to Eli.

Finally, Eli figured out what was happening. God was calling the boy. Eli told Samuel how to answer.

The next time, Samuel was ready. "Speak, Lord," he said, "for Your servant is listening."

96

Samuel, the Prophet

1 SAMUEL 3:11–21

God told Samuel, "Eli's grown sons are wicked, and Eli lets them get away with it. So I am going to punish Eli's family. Later, when people hear of it, their ears will tingle."

Samuel lay there until morning. He was afraid to tell Eli what God had said to him. He got up and went into the tabernacle.

"Samuel, my son," Eli called.

"Here I am."

"What did the Lord tell you last night? Don't hide anything from me." So Samuel told Eli everything he had heard.

"It is the Lord," said Eli. "Let Him do what is good in His eyes."

As Samuel grew, God was with him. Everything he said had meaning. All the Israelites knew Samuel. "He is a prophet—a person who speaks for God—and he can be trusted," they said.

97
The Lost Ark of the Covenant
1 SAMUEL 4:1–22

God punished Eli's family just as He said He would. The Philistines made war with the Israelites, and many were killed. The Israelites didn't know that God was punishing Eli's relatives. "Why did God let the Philistines win?" they wondered. "Let's bring God's ark of the covenant with us. Then God will be among us and will save us."

Eli's sons had the job of taking good care of the ark, but instead they carried it into battle. While the Israelites fought the Philistines, the enemy stole the ark, and Eli's sons died in the fight.

Eli sat at the city gate waiting, worried sick about the ark. A man raced from the battle with the news: "Your sons are dead. The ark is captured!" Hearing this, Eli fell over backward and died. Because the ark was captured, God's goodness went away from Israel.

98
Israel Asks for a King
1 SAMUEL 8:1–22

Samuel became a judge who ruled Israel. In time, the Philistines returned the ark, and there was peace. The people were serving God again, but now they wanted a king. "Choose a king for us like other nations have," they told Samuel.

This made Samuel unhappy. He worried a king would turn Israel away from God. Then God said to Samuel, "Do what they want. They're leaving Me, not you. They've been turning against Me ever since coming out of Egypt."

Samuel warned the people, "A king will tell you what to do. A king will take your daughters and sons to be servants and soldiers. A king will cause trouble and make you cry."

Still, the people said, "We want to be like the other nations."

So God said to Samuel, "Give them a king."

99
God Chooses Israel's King
1 SAMUEL 9:1–25

God told Samuel, "A man will come from Benjamin. Make him king of Israel. He'll save my people from the Philistines."

Saul, a young man from Benjamin's tribe, and his servant were out searching for lost donkeys when the servant said, "A prophet lives in this town. He may know where they are."

When Samuel saw Saul walking up the hill, God spoke again. "This is the man I told you about."

"Where does the prophet live?" Saul asked Samuel.

"I'm the prophet," Samuel answered. He invited Saul inside to eat. "Do you know that all Israel will put its hope in you?"

"My family is the smallest in the tribe of Benjamin," said Saul. "Why do you say Israel will put its hope in me?"

Samuel provided Saul with a great feast. He was given the best seat. His food was the finest of all that was served.

100
Samuel Anoints Israel's King
1 SAMUEL 9:26–10:27

In the morning, Samuel and Saul walked together from the town. Samuel sent Saul's servant on ahead. "Saul," Samuel said, "God has told me to anoint you king to rule over Israel." Then Samuel poured olive oil from a small bottle onto Saul's head. This was a special ceremony to celebrate Saul's service to God. "This is how you will know what I've told you is true. As you travel, you'll come to Rachel's tomb. There, two men will say, 'Your donkeys have been found. Now your father is looking for you.' "

It happened just as Samuel said. After three hundred years of being ruled by judges, Israel had a king.

101
Samuel Gives the Kingdom to Saul
1 SAMUEL 11:1–12:25

Israel's enemy, the Ammonites, attacked them. All of Israel cried, and Saul heard them. The anger he felt was like fire. Saul sent his oxen around Israel to send a message: "Join me to fight the Ammonites." More than three hundred thousand joined Saul in the fight, and the Ammonites ran away.

Samuel was pleased when he saw what Saul did. Then Samuel gave the Israelite kingdom to Saul. Samuel said goodbye to the people. "I'll always pray for you," he said. "Serve the Lord faithfully. Don't be wicked again. If you are, you and your king will be swept away."

102
Saul Makes an Offering
1 SAMUEL 13:1–14

The Philistines still caused trouble for the Israelites. Saul blew his trumpet—a signal calling the Israelites to war. Many came, but they were afraid.

Samuel sent a message to Saul. "I will come and make an offering to God. Wait seven days until I come and show you what you should do."

Saul waited seven days, but Samuel was late. So Saul made his own offering to God.

When Samuel arrived, he said, "What have you done?"

"My men were scattering," Saul answered. "I thought the enemy might attack. So I made the offering myself."

"You have not done what I said, and you have not kept the Lord's commands," said Samuel. "If you had waited and trusted God, you'd be safe. But now God will find some other man to do His will. This other man will seek the Lord's heart. Someday, God will take the kingdom from you and give it to him."

103
God Rips Away the Kingdom
1 SAMUEL 15:1–35

Saul and his army defeated the Philistines and all of Israel's enemies. Finally, there was peace.

But God wanted His Amalekite enemies destroyed too, along with everything they owned. So Saul's army destroyed their city. But Saul kept the animals as gifts for God.

When Samuel found out that Saul had disobeyed again, he said, "God wants your obedience more than your gifts. He has rejected you as king."

Saul grabbed Samuel's robe and ripped it. Then Samuel spoke to Saul for the last time: "Today God has ripped your kingdom from you and given it to a better man."

104
David, the Anointed Boy
1 SAMUEL 16:1–12

God told Samuel, "Bring oil to Bethlehem and anoint Jesse's son as Israel's new king." Samuel went to Bethlehem and gave an offering to God.

The man, Jesse, and seven of his sons were there.

Samuel thought, *I'll anoint one of these strong young men.* But God said, "They look good, but I don't want them. People only see what others look like. I look at their hearts."

"Do you have another son?" Samuel asked Jesse.

"My youngest son, David, is with the sheep."

Jesse sent for David. When the boy arrived, God said to Samuel, "Pick him. This is the one."

105
David, the Musician-King
1 SAMUEL 16:13–23

David was about fifteen years old, with bright eyes and rosy cheeks. Samuel anointed him with oil as his older brothers watched. God's Spirit was with David from that day on.

Meanwhile, King Saul was not at peace with God. In his heart, he felt gloomy.

Because David played the harp well, Jesse sent him to Saul. Saul's servants thought the music would help cheer the king. Saul loved David's music. It made the king feel better. But Saul didn't know that Samuel had anointed David. The boy who played the harp for Saul was Israel's future king.

106
David, the Shepherd-Warrior
1 SAMUEL 17:1–45

While Saul was still king, the Philistines were at war with Israel. The Philistines had a giant soldier named Goliath. He stood nine feet tall. Goliath dared the Israelites to fight, but they were too afraid.

David, the shepherd boy, wasn't afraid. "Who is this big guy?" he asked the Israelites. "Don't let him get in your way!" Holding his shepherd's staff in his hand, David went to fight Goliath. From a stream, he picked up five stones for his slingshot. Then David walked toward Goliath. "You come with a sword. I come in the name of the Lord," David said.

107

David Fights Goliath

1 SAMUEL 17:46–52

Goliath saw that David held a shepherd's staff. "You're here to fight me with a stick?" Goliath laughed.

"God is with me!" David shouted. "I'll knock you down. Then the Philistines will be defeated, and the world will know God watches over Israel."

David and Goliath rushed toward each other. David put his hand into his bag, took out a stone, and fired it with his slingshot. It hit Goliath. The stone went into his forehead so hard that Goliath fell on his face to the ground.

That day, David won a great victory for Israel.

108
David, King on the Run
1 SAMUEL 17:57–22:5

After defeating Goliath and the Philistines, David became a leader in King Saul's army. Saul loved David until David became the best at everything he did and everyone liked him. This made the king jealous. He wanted David gone. And one day, David even had to jump from his window to escape the king's anger.

A few men ran away with David. They all stopped at the tabernacle, where they were given some bread to eat. There, David saw Goliath's sword, and he took it. David and his men hid in the caves in a place called Judah. Four hundred men joined David there, and he became their captain. David would keep hiding until King Saul died.

109
David Spares Saul's Life
1 SAMUEL 24:1–22

King Saul went looking for David but could not find him. While David was hiding in the darkness of one of the caves, he noticed Saul was outside. Saul was alone and had stopped to rest there for a while.

"Here's your chance," David's men whispered to him. "Now you can kill your enemy, the king."

"I will not harm him," David said. Instead, David quietly crawled out of the cave and cut a corner from the king's cloak while he slept.

Saul woke up.

"My lord, the king," David said, waving the piece of cloth. "This proves I don't want to harm you."

Then Saul began to cry. "May God reward you with good," he said. "I know now that you will be the next king of Israel."

110
Saul Seeks Samuel's Spirit
1 SAMUEL 28:3–19; 31:1–12; 2 SAMUEL 1:1–27

Years passed. King Saul was old and sick. The Philistines had a huge army ready to fight Israel, and Saul didn't know what to do. He was afraid. Saul prayed to God but got no answer. Then he went and found a woman who said she could see things that would happen in the future.

Samuel had died years before, but Saul said to the woman, "Bring me Samuel's spirit."

God allowed Samuel's spirit to come to Saul.

"What shall I do?" Saul asked. "The Philistines are at war, and God won't answer me."

Samuel said, "I told you that God has ripped the kingdom from you. Tomorrow will be a bad day for you."

The next day, the Philistines attacked. Saul died in the battle. David was far away, but when he got the news, he cried because the king and his soldiers were dead.

111
David, the Conquering King
2 SAMUEL 5:1–25

After King Saul died, David did not become king right away. Some Israelites thought the next king should be someone from Saul's family. Seven years passed. Then, finally, Israel made David their king. He was thirty years old.

The Philistines still had a huge army, and again, they were ready to attack and camped in a nearby valley.

David prayed.

"Go around behind them," God answered. "You'll hear a marching sound in the treetops. This means I've gone into battle ahead of you. I'll strike down the Philistines' army."

David obeyed God, and that day, his army defeated the Philistines.

112
David, the Joyful Dancer
2 SAMUEL 6:1–23

When Saul had ruled Israel, he hid away the ark of the covenant. David decided it was time to bring it to Jerusalem. He had a special cart built to carry the ark. As it rolled toward the city, David and other Israelites followed behind it. They sang joyful songs, made music, and danced.

There was a tabernacle in a place called Mount Zion. The priests carried the ark into the tabernacle and made offerings there to God. All of Israel shouted with joy, and David danced to honor Him.

113

David's Heart for God

2 SAMUEL 7:1–29

Jerusalem became known as the City of David, and David made sure that God was worshipped properly. Priests offered gifts to God in the tent that was the tabernacle.

David lived in a beautiful house, but God's ark stayed in the tent. One day, David said to the prophet Nathan, "I live in a beautiful home, yet God's ark is in a tent."

Then God spoke His words to Nathan. "My ark has always been in the meeting tent. No one except David has ever thought of building Me a beautiful house. David loves Me in his heart. Tell David, 'I gave you a great name and great power. Now I will give you a kingdom. Your son will sit on the throne after you die. He will build a house for Me. You and your children and their families will have the kingdom. It will last forever.'"

114
David's Wicked Plan
2 SAMUEL 11:1–27

As a new king, David went into battle with his warriors. But as the years went on, he stayed in his palace when his army went to fight.

One day, David saw a beautiful woman in a nearby garden. "Who is she?" David asked his servant.

"Her name is Bathsheba. She's the wife of Uriah, one of your soldiers," the servant said.

David fell in love with Bathsheba, but they couldn't get married because she was already married to Uriah. Then David made a wicked plan. He sent Uriah into a battle and put him in the front lines where the fighting was worst. Uriah was killed!

Then David sent for Bathsheba. He brought her into his house and married her. They had a baby. David loved the child. But God was displeased with what David had done.

115
"You Are That Man!"
2 SAMUEL 12:1–14

God gave Nathan a story to tell King David: "There were two men, one rich and one poor. The rich man had many flocks of sheep. The poor man had just one lamb. A visitor came to the rich man's house for dinner. The man didn't want to kill one of his own sheep for the meal, so instead, he robbed the poor man of his one lamb."

"That's terrible!" David said. "That man should be punished."

"You are that man!" said Nathan. "God made you king. You have everything, but you killed Uriah. You and your family will suffer because of it."

116
Trouble Comes to David
2 SAMUEL 3:2–3; 12:13–25

Nathan, the prophet, had said suffering would come to David because of what he did to Uriah. Soon bad things began to happen. David and Bathsheba's baby boy got sick. David cried and asked God to make the child well. But it didn't happen. David and Bathsheba had other sons. One of them was named Solomon. Nathan called him a different name: Jedidiah, which means "loved by God." Many of David's sons grew up wild and wicked. One was David's third-oldest son, Absalom, a handsome man with beautiful, long hair.

117
David, on the Run Again
2 SAMUEL 13:1–15:23

There was much trouble in David's house. Absalom was angry with his brother Amnon. One day, at a feast when David's sons were together, Absalom's servants got rid of Amnon. Absalom ran and hid at his grandparents' house. The other boys ran to their dad. When David heard what had happened, he was very sad.

Absalom wanted to be king and become powerful in Israel. After three years of hiding, he returned. He gathered with others like he was joining in worship, but instead he had himself named king of Israel. David heard that everyone in Israel loved Absalom, and this made David afraid. He told his family, "Let's run, or we'll never escape from Absalom." Some of the Israelites cried when they saw King David and his family running away into the desert.

118
"My Son! My Son!"
2 SAMUEL 17:24–18:33

David hid in a place called Gilead. He gathered an army together. Although it wasn't big like Absalom's, David's army was brave. As they marched to battle with Absalom, David said, "Be gentle with Absalom. He is my son."

The battle was fierce. Absalom's army was losing, so Absalom rode off on his horse trying to escape. His long hair caught on a tree branch, and he was left hanging there. A messenger came to David to let him know his son was dead.

"O my son, Absalom," David cried. "I wish I had died instead of you. My son! My son!"

119
Sad David
2 SAMUEL 19:1–8

David's soldiers heard that the king was sad about Absalom. The great victory that should have been a celebration instead turned to sadness. David put his hands over his face. "O my son, Absalom, O Absalom, my son, my son!"

Joab, the commander of King David's army, went to David and said, "This army has saved your life. Your sons and daughters and wives are all safe. You act like you loved Absalom, the one who hated you. Don't you care about the ones who love you? Speak kindly to your army. If you don't, I'm sure more trouble will come to you."

So David went out and spoke kind words to his troops.

120
The Place of God's House

2 SAMUEL 24:1–25; 1 CHRONICLES 21:1–27

David's kingdom stretched almost as far as eyes could see. David did something that upset God. He sent his commander, Joab, to count all the people in the kingdom. God did not tell David to do this. Joab knew it was wrong. But he had to obey his king.

Because David disobeyed God, more trouble came. A disease spread through the kingdom. Then an angel ordered David to give an offering at the place where Abraham had built an altar long ago.

David made an offering there to God. Then David said, "This is the place where we'll build God's house. Israel's altar for offerings will be right here."

121
Preparing for God's House
1 KINGS 1:1–53; 1 CHRONICLES 22:1–19

David wanted to build God's temple, but God said, "David, you have been a man of war. I want a peaceful man to build My house. After you die, your son Solomon will be king. There will be peace, and he'll build My house."

David gathered all the materials for the building. "Solomon," he told his son, "God promised peace while you are king. He'll be with you, and you'll build His house."

When David became old, another of his sons, Adonijah, decided he wanted to be the next king. David didn't want this! Instead, he said, "Today, I make Solomon king."

Solomon became king, and the people celebrated so loudly the ground shook.

Solomon and his brother Adonijah made peace with each other. "If you are honorable, we will get along," King Solomon said.

122
Solomon Prays for Wisdom
1 KINGS 3:3–15

Solomon's kingdom was strong, and Israel was at peace. One night, the Lord came to Solomon in a dream. "What would you like Me to give you?" God asked.

Solomon answered, "I am only a young man, Lord. I don't know how to rule this great people. Give me wisdom and knowledge to know right and wrong."

God was pleased. "You didn't ask for a long life or for riches or power. Instead, you've asked for wisdom to rule My people. So I will give you more wisdom than any other king. No other ruler will ever have more wisdom than you. And because you've asked only for this, I'll give you even more. Obey My words like your father, David, obeyed. Then you'll have a long life and rule for many years."

123
Solomon's Wisdom
1 KINGS 3:16–28

Solomon judged matters both great and small.

One day, two women came to him with one baby. One woman pointed at the other and said, "Her baby died, and she switched it for mine!"

"That's not true!" said the other. "This is *my* baby!"

The women continued to argue in front of Solomon until he said, "Enough! What if we divide the baby in two and you each get half?"

The first woman stopped arguing and said, "Let her have the baby. Don't hurt my son."

Solomon had known just what to say to find out which woman was the real mother. It was wisdom like this that made all of Israel in awe of their king.

124
God's Temple Is Built
1 KINGS 5:1–8:66

The most important thing Solomon did was build God's temple at a place called Mount Moriah in Jerusalem.

The temple was designed much like the tabernacle, only much larger. This new place of worship was not a tent. It was strongly built of stone and cedarwood. The stones for the walls were cut to fit just right. The cedar posts and beams were perfectly carved and then brought to Jerusalem. Building the temple took seven years. Then the ark of the covenant was placed in God's special room there, the Holy of Holies. When the temple was complete, King Solomon and the Israelites worshipped there.

125
Solomon's Kingdom Part One
1 KINGS 9:1–9

God said to Solomon, "I have made the temple holy. It will be My house. Do as your father, David, did, and follow Me. Then your kingdom will last forever. But if you stop following Me, I'll let Israel's enemies destroy the temple you've built for Me."

Solomon's palace stood just below the temple. It had so many cedar pillars that they looked like a forest.

Israel was greater than ever under King Solomon. Many countries sent their princes to visit him and see his riches. They were amazed at his wisdom and understanding. Some said he was the wisest man in the world. Solomon wrote many of his wise sayings in the book of Proverbs. It is said that he wrote one thousand songs.

126
The Queen of Sheba
1 KINGS 10:1–13

Sheba was a land far away, a thousand miles from Israel. When the queen of Sheba heard of Solomon's wisdom, she went to visit him. The queen brought expensive gifts with her. While they were together, she asked Solomon many hard questions. Solomon answered them all. He showed her his beautiful palace: his throne, his servants, his food, and the steps from his palace up to the temple.

"Everything I've heard of your wisdom and greatness is true," the queen said. "The Lord, who has set you on Israel's throne, is blessed." After she gave Solomon the treasures she had brought, the queen returned to Sheba.

127
Solomon's Kingdom Part Two
1 KINGS 10:14–11:13

While living in his palace with all its beautiful things, King Solomon began not caring about the poor people in his kingdom. He made them pay taxes so he could buy even more nice things. The people cried because their lives were so hard.

The king didn't love God with his whole heart. Solomon had many wives. They worshipped idols, and to make his wives happy, Solomon built a temple for their false gods. Soon, statues of false gods were all over Jerusalem, and Solomon offered gifts to them.

This made God angry. "I'm going to rip the kingdom from you," He said. "But not while you live. I'll give it to your servant. I'll rip it away from your son. Only one tribe will be left in Israel. Your son will rule it because your father, David, loved Me."

128
Israel Is Divided
1 KINGS 11:42–12:20

After Solomon died, his son, Rehoboam, sat on the throne. But Rehoboam was weak. Solomon's servant, Jeroboam, led the Israelites. The people said to Rehoboam, "You can be our king if you stop ruling like your father, overworking us and making us pay taxes."

"I'll let you know," Rehoboam said.

Rehoboam went to his father's wise old men for advice. "Do what they ask," the men said.

Then Rehoboam talked to the young princes of Israel. "How shall I answer the people?" he asked.

"Tell them you're much stronger than your father," they advised.

Rehoboam ignored the old men's advice. He did what the young princes said. And that day, ten of Israel's tribes rebelled against Rehoboam and made Solomon's servant, Jeroboam, their king. Jeroboam ruled the ten tribes in northern Israel. Rehoboam was king over the tribe of Judah and part of Benjamin's in southern Israel.

129
The Sin of Jeroboam
1 KINGS 12:25–13:5

Jeroboam worried that his people might turn against him because all of Israel, both north and south, worshipped in Jerusalem where Rehoboam led. So he made two gold statues that looked like calves. "Here are your gods," he said to his people. "They rescued you from Egypt." Of course, this wasn't true. The one real God had rescued them. Jeroboam caused God's people to worship idols, and this has been called "the sin of Jeroboam" ever since.

While Jeroboam was worshipping at the altar of a false god, a prophet spoke God's words to him. "A man will come from David's family named Josiah. He will destroy the priests who worship false gods. Here is the proof: The altar will break down. Its ashes will spill out—"

Just then, Jeroboam tried to grab the prophet. Instantly, Jeroboam's hand shriveled up. The altar broke apart, and its ashes spilled out.

130
God Punishes Jeroboam
1 KINGS 14:1–20

Jeroboam's son was sick. The king told the boy's mother, "Disguise yourself. No one must know you're my wife. Go ask the prophet Ahijah if the child will get well."

This is what the prophet told her: "God says, 'Tell the king I made you the leader of My people. I ripped the kingdom away from David's family for you. But you have done more evil than any other king. I'm very angry because you made false gods. I will allow trouble to come to you.' "

The prophet sent Jeroboam's wife away. And trouble did come to Israel. The people scattered far away because of the sin of Jeroboam. After King Jeroboam died, his son, Nadab, became the new king.

131
So Many Kings!
1 KINGS 15:27–16:33

The trouble in Israel continued. Many kings followed Nadab. The next was Baasha, one of Nadab's servants. He made himself king! When Baasha died, his son, Elah, was king. But that didn't work out when his servant, Zimri, rebelled against him and took over the palace. Then a man named Omri took over, and Zimri burned the palace down.

Omri became Israel's next king. Like the kings before him, Omri worshipped idols. Still, he stayed in power for a while. King Omri built a city called Samaria for the Israelites, and he made peace with the people of Judah's tribe who lived in Jerusalem.

After Omri, there came the worst king of all—Ahab. His wife, Jezebel, was evil. She hunted down and destroyed God's prophets.

132
God's Prophet Elijah
1 KINGS 17:1–7

When Ahab was king, a great prophet—a man who spoke God's words—came from a place called Gilead. His name was Elijah.

Elijah spoke these words to King Ahab: "God lives, and I am with Him. There won't be any rain or even dew on your land until I say so." Then Elijah went away to a place called Cherith Creek.

God said to Elijah, "When you're thirsty, drink from the creek. I've commanded the ravens to feed you when you're hungry."

Morning and evening, ravens brought Elijah meat and bread. He drank from the creek. But soon the creek dried up because no rain fell on the land.

133
Elijah and the Widow of Zarephath
1 KINGS 17:8–18

God told Elijah, "Go to a place called Zarephath. A widow there will feed you." Elijah obeyed God. He found the widow near the gate gathering firewood.

"Bring me a little water," Elijah told her. "Will you bring me a bit of bread too?"

The widow answered, "If I bake bread, all my flour and oil will be gone. My son and I will starve."

"Make bread for me," Elijah said. "God says: 'Your flour and oil will last until rain comes again.' " The widow believed him. The jar that held her flour was never empty. The jug of oil didn't run out. Everything happened exactly as Elijah had said it would.

But then the widow's son got sick. She worried he would die. "Man of God, do you have something against me?" she cried to Elijah. "Did God send you to punish me because of my sin?"

134
The Little Boy Lives
1 KINGS 17:19–24

The widow's son died. Elijah carried the boy to his room. "O God!" Elijah prayed. "Is this what You want to happen to the widow and her son?" Then Elijah lay down on the boy and cried out to God, "Let the boy live!" God answered Elijah's prayer, and the little boy was alive again. Elijah brought him to his mother. "See. Your son lives."

The widow said to Elijah, "Now I'm sure you are a man of God. You speak His words in truth."

135
A Test
1 KINGS 18:1–29

After three years without rain, God told Elijah, "Go visit Ahab. I'm going to send rain."

On the way, Elijah met Obadiah. Obadiah was the man in charge of King Ahab's palace. Obadiah was looking for grass for the animals. "Tell the king I'm here," Elijah said.

When King Ahab saw Elijah, he said, "Aren't you the one who brought trouble to Israel?"

Elijah answered, "You caused it not to rain, Ahab, because you worship false gods.

Elijah answered, "You caused it not to rain, Ahab, because you worship false gods. Choose: false gods or the real God. Bring two oxen as gifts—one for the priests who worship false gods and one for me. We'll put them on two altars and do a test. You call to your god. I'll call to mine. The altar that catches on fire shows who Israel's one true God is."

The priests went first. They placed their offering and firewood on their altar and called to their god all morning, but nothing happened.

136
The One True God
1 KINGS 18:30–39

Elijah made his altar of twelve stones to represent the twelve tribes of Israel. He placed his offering and firewood on top. Then Elijah dug a ditch around his altar. Three times he ordered water to pour over the altar. And it happened! Everything was soaked, and the ditch filled with water. Elijah prayed, "O God of Abraham, Isaac, and Israel, show them that You are Israel's God. Turn their hearts back to You." Suddenly, fire came out of the sky and burned up the offering.

When the people saw this, they fell down shouting, "This is the one true God!"

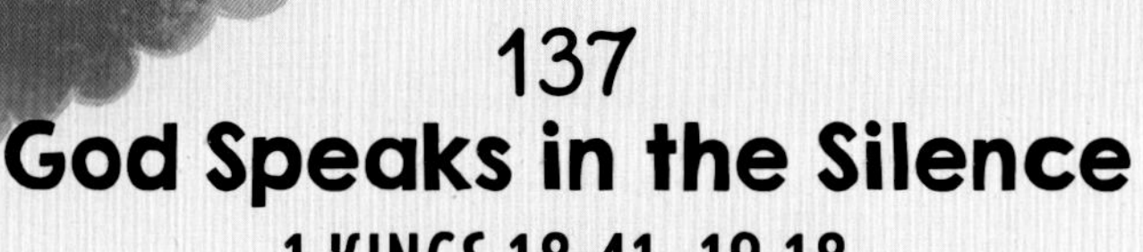

137
God Speaks in the Silence
1 KINGS 18:41–19:18

King Ahab was amazed. "When Elijah prayed, it rained!" he said. His wife, Jezebel, who trusted false gods, was angry, and she wanted to hurt Elijah.

Poor Elijah ran for his life. Finally, he was so tired he fell asleep under a tree. An angel touched him. "Wake up and eat, Elijah." Nearby was hot bread and cool water. Elijah ate, then he traveled forty days to a cave in Mount Horeb.

"O God," he prayed. "The Israelites have turned against You, and they want to destroy me."

"Go up on the mountain," God said. "I'm going to pass by."

The wind blew so strong it shattered the rocks. But God wasn't in the wind. Then came an earthquake. God wasn't there. Then fire. God wasn't in the fire. Finally, in the silence God spoke: "There will be seven thousand in Israel who haven't worshipped a false god."

138
Elijah Finds Elisha
1 KINGS 19:15–21

God told Elijah, "Find Elisha and make him a prophet. Then make Hazael king of Syria and make Jehu king of Israel. A war will happen between Hazael's and Jehu's people. Seven thousand people will be left. They are the ones who haven't worshipped a false god."

Elijah found Elisha. He put his cape over Elisha's shoulders, making him a prophet. Before he left to follow Elijah, Elisha made a huge feast, and the people nearby ate the meat of two oxen. Then Elisha followed Elijah down the path, wearing the great prophet's cape. Elisha became Elijah's servant.

139

The Stolen Vineyard

1 KINGS 21:1–29

Next to King Ahab's palace was a vineyard belonging to a man named Naboth. "Let me buy your vineyard," said the king. "I want to plant vegetables there."

"This vineyard was my great-grandfather's," Naboth replied. "I won't sell."

When Jezebel found out her husband, the king, couldn't have the vineyard, she carried out a plan to destroy Naboth. After that, she said to Ahab, "Take Naboth's vineyard. He's gone."

While Ahab and Jezebel walked in the vineyard they'd stolen, Elijah appeared. "God will make your family like Jeroboam's," he told the king. "They'll be destroyed for what you've done. As for you, Jezebel, you will be destroyed too and given to the dogs!"

140

Elijah's Final Journey

2 KINGS 2:1–8

Ahab's family was destroyed, just as God said.

Meanwhile, Elijah's work in Israel was done. Soon, he would go to be with God.

Elisha didn't want to leave Elijah, but Elijah said, "Stay here. God wants me to go to the Jordan River." Elisha refused to stay. They walked to the river together while fifty of Elijah's followers stood nearby watching.

At the river, Elijah took off his cape. He rolled it up, and he hit the water with it. The Jordan River divided, and Elijah and Elisha crossed it on dry ground.

141
Elijah Leaves in a Whirlwind
2 KINGS 2:9–12

"Tell me, Elisha, what can I do for you before I'm taken to be with God?" Elijah asked.

"Please give me a double share of your spirit," Elisha said. He saw how God had done great things while using Elijah's spirit, and Elisha wanted the same for himself—he wanted God to work through him even more—a double portion.

"You are asking a lot," said Elijah. "But if you see me as I'm taken away, it's yours."

Suddenly, a chariot of fire pulled by flaming horses came between the two men. Elijah was flown away in a whirlwind into heaven.

Elisha watched. "Elijah! Elijah!" he cried. "The chariot of God and its horsemen!" But Elijah was out of sight.

142
"Elisha Has Elijah's Spirit"
2 KINGS 2:13–22

Elijah's cape lay nearby. It had fallen from his shoulders during the whirlwind. Elisha picked it up and stood on the riverbank. He took the cape and hit the water with it. Again, the river divided, and Elisha walked across on dry land.

Elijah's followers were waiting. "Elisha has Elijah's spirit!" they said when they saw the river divide.

Word spread that Elisha had been given Elijah's power. People from Jericho came to Elisha the prophet. They said, "The water in our spring is bad."

"Bring me a new bottle and fill it with salt," Elisha told them. He threw the salt into the spring. "The Lord says, 'I have made this water healthy. No sickness or death will come from it again.' " And Jericho's water became perfect.

143
God Works through Elisha
2 KINGS 4:1–7

With God working through him, Elisha had power to do amazing things. One day, a woman came to him and said, "My husband died. He owed people a lot of money, and now they want to take everything I have."

"Do you have anything to pay them?" Elisha asked.

"All I have is one jar of oil," she said.

"Borrow as many empty jars as you can. Then fill them," Elisha told her.

The neighbors brought jars, and the woman kept pouring oil from her jar. It never ran out! Every jar she could find was filled with oil.

"Now sell the oil and pay your debts," the prophet said.

This and many other things Elisha did showed Israel that Elisha was God's prophet.

144
Elisha Cures a Skin Disease
2 KINGS 5:1–27

Naaman, an army commander, had a terrible skin disease called leprosy. "The prophet Elisha could cure you," one of his wife's helpers suggested.

On his way to Elisha's house, Naaman was met by Elisha's servant. "Elisha says, 'Naaman, wash in the Jordan River seven times. Your skin will become pure.' "

"Why didn't Elisha tell me himself?" Naaman complained. He was ready to walk away when the servant spoke again. "All Elisha said was 'Wash, and be clean.' So why not do it?"

Naaman went to the river and bathed seven times. The skin disease left him. His skin became perfect like a baby's! Then Naaman went to Elisha and said, "Now I'm sure there is a God." He offered Elisha an expensive gift, but Elisha refused to take it.

145
Israel's Chariots of Fire
2 KINGS 6:8–23

Syria's and Israel's armies were at war. Israel always seemed to know ahead of time what Syria's army would do. "There must be a spy in our camp," said Syria's king.

"There's no spy," his men said. "Israel has Elisha, the prophet."

So, the king sent his army to capture Elisha. "There are horses and chariots all around us!" Elisha's servant cried. "Master, what should we do?"

"Don't be afraid," Elisha told him. "There are more with us than there are with them. Lord," Elisha prayed, "please help my servant see." Suddenly, the servant saw God's horses and chariots of fire all around. "Now, please strike Syria's army blind," Elisha prayed.

Then Elisha led the blinded Syrian army into Israel, where he advised Israel's king to let them go.

146

Food for the Samaritans

2 KINGS 6:24–7:11

Syria's army surrounded the city of Samaria, and the people there were starving. Elisha told their king, "Don't give up. Tomorrow the people will have enough food."

A nobleman, one of Samaria's most important men, didn't believe Elisha. "Only if food rains from heaven," he said.

"You'll see it with your eyes, but you won't eat any," Elisha answered.

That night, God caused the Syrian soldiers to hear a huge army approaching. They ran from their camp and left everything behind—even their food. Four men found the camp empty and unguarded. Then they ran to Samaria to share the good news.

147
The Nobleman Gets No Food
2 KINGS 7:12–20

When the news came to Samaria, a crowd waited by the city gate. They waited there for food from the Syrian camp.

The king chose a man to guard the gate. He chose the nobleman, the one who had laughed and said to Elisha, "Only if food rains from heaven."

Remember what Elisha said in reply? "You'll see it with your eyes, but you won't eat any," he had promised.

The nobleman discovered that Elisha was right. When the people saw the food coming, there was more than enough for all of them, just as Elisha had said. The Samaritan people were starving. They ran to the city gate to get the food. But the nobleman ate none of it. He was knocked to the ground by the crowd.

148
Hazael Becomes Syria's King
2 KINGS 8:7–15

Before Elijah had gone to heaven, he'd told Elisha to anoint two kings: Hazael, king of Syria, and Jehu, king of Israel.

When Elisha went to Syria, a king named Ben-hadad was in power. He was sick. Hazael was an official in the king's court. "Ask the prophet Elisha if I'll get well," Ben-hadad said.

"The king will get well," Elisha told Hazael, and then Elisha cried.

"Why are you crying?" Hazael asked.

"Because you will become the next king of Syria, and you will do terrible things," Elisha answered.

Elisha was right again. Hazael returned to King Ben-hadad and said, "The prophet says you will get well." The next day Hazael came into the king's bedroom, and while the king slept, Hazael took the king's bedspread and covered the king's face. Then Hazael became Syria's new king.

149
Jehu Becomes Israel's King
2 KINGS 9:1–13

In Israel, Elisha told his helper, a young prophet, "Take this oil. Find the army captain named Jehu. Then say to him, 'The Lord says I have anointed you king of Israel.' When you've done this, return to me."

The young prophet found several captains sitting together in Israel's camp. "I have a message for you, Commander," he said.

"For which of us?" Jehu asked.

"For you, sir." The prophet poured oil on Jehu's head. "The Lord God says this: 'I have anointed you as king over My people, the Israelites. You must destroy the family of Ahab your king. This is how I will punish Jezebel for destroying so many of My people.' " Then the prophet left.

"I've just been made king over Israel," Jehu said in disbelief.

The captains threw their robes down in front of him. A trumpet blared, and they all shouted, "Jehu is king!"

150
"It's a Trick!"
2 KINGS 9:16–23

Judah's king Ahaziah was in a place called Jezreel visiting his brother King Joram of Israel. Both were Ahab and Jezebel's sons. The king's watchman reported, "I see a company of our soldiers coming in a hurry. I think Jehu is leading them. Maybe he has news of the battle with Syria." Both kings set out in their chariots, hoping for news. When they reached Jehu, King Joram asked, "Do you come in peace?"

"There will be no peace as long as your mother, Jezebel, worships her false gods and does other evil things!" Jehu answered.

King Joram shouted to his brother, "It's a trick!" Then the kings turned their chariots around and tried to get away.

151
Ahab's Family—Gone!
2 KINGS 9:23–10:30

"It's a trick, Ahaziah!" Joram cried as he rode off in his chariot. But Jehu was close behind. He overpowered Joram, destroying him.

King Ahaziah took off in the other direction, but Jehu and his men caught up with Ahaziah too, and he was destroyed.

When Jezebel heard both her sons were gone, she put on her crown and makeup and waited for Jehu and his men to show up. When they did, Jezebel asked, "Did you come in peace?"

"No!" Jehu shouted. Then Jezebel fell to the ground from her palace window, and dogs carried her away.

Ahab's whole family was destroyed just as God had commanded, and God was pleased. "Your sons will rule Israel," God told Jehu. "Your great-grandson will one day be king."

152
Elisha's Life-Giving Bones
2 KINGS 13:14–25

When Elisha was old and ready to die, Jehu's grandson, Joash, was king. "Elisha! Don't go!" The king put his hands over his face and cried. "We need you to help defeat our enemies."

"Pick up your bow and arrows," Elisha told him. "Open the window and shoot." The king pulled back the bowstring and shot. "This is God's arrow of victory over your enemy, Syria," Elisha said. Then he told the king to shoot arrows into the ground. Joash shot three times. "Why did you stop?" Elisha asked. "You should have hit the ground five or six times. Then you would have had that many victories. Now your army will beat Syria's three times and no more."

After Elisha died and was buried in a cave, another man was buried in the same place. When his body touched Elisha's bones, the man came back to life!

153
Jonah Runs from God
JONAH 1:1–11

Israel had a new enemy, Assyria. Its capital city, Nineveh, was filled with people doing evil things. God told a man named Jonah, "Go to Nineveh. Warn its people. I know of their wickedness."

Jonah didn't obey God. Instead, he got on a ship and sailed away. So God sent a great wind and a mighty storm to put the ship in danger. Its sailors began throwing cargo overboard to lighten the load. Meanwhile, Jonah was below deck, sound asleep. "How can you sleep!" the sailors cried. "Call on your God to save us! We must find the man who caused this."

"I'm the one," Jonah confessed. "I'm running from God."

This made the sailors even more afraid. "No wonder this is happening," they said.

154

Jonah and the Big Fish

JONAH 1:11–2:10

"What shall we do to calm the sea?" the sailors asked.

"Throw me overboard," said Jonah. "I've caused all this trouble."

The sailors tried rowing the ship to shore. But that didn't work. There was nothing else they could do, so the men prayed for forgiveness and threw Jonah into the sea.

Immediately, the storm stopped. The sea became calm. A huge fish came along, and in one big gulp, it swallowed Jonah! He sat inside its belly for three days and nights, praying to God. Finally, God spoke to the fish, and it spit Jonah out onto a nearby beach.

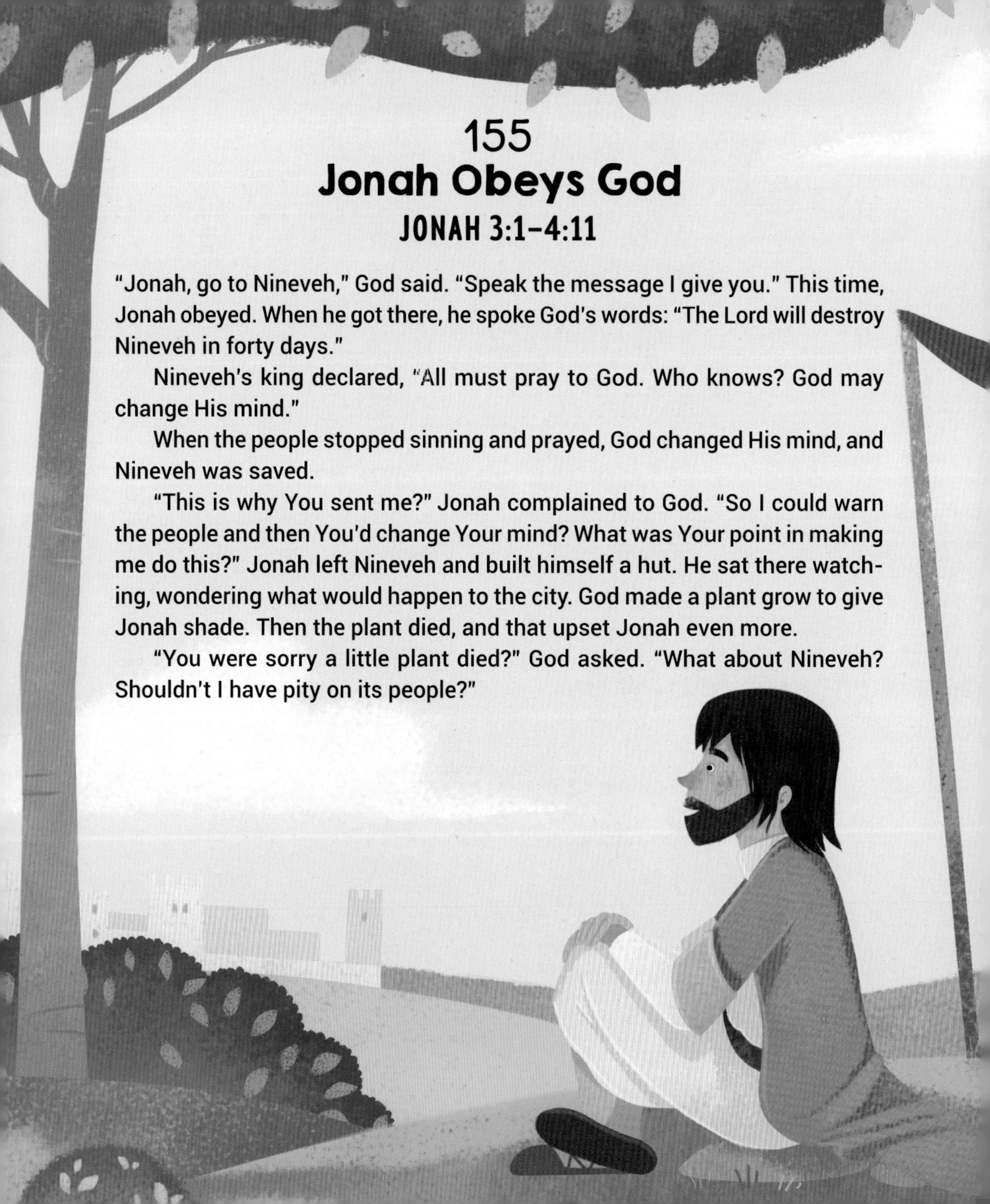

155
Jonah Obeys God
JONAH 3:1–4:11

"Jonah, go to Nineveh," God said. "Speak the message I give you." This time, Jonah obeyed. When he got there, he spoke God's words: "The Lord will destroy Nineveh in forty days."

Nineveh's king declared, "All must pray to God. Who knows? God may change His mind."

When the people stopped sinning and prayed, God changed His mind, and Nineveh was saved.

"This is why You sent me?" Jonah complained to God. "So I could warn the people and then You'd change Your mind? What was Your point in making me do this?" Jonah left Nineveh and built himself a hut. He sat there watching, wondering what would happen to the city. God made a plant grow to give Jonah shade. Then the plant died, and that upset Jonah even more.

"You were sorry a little plant died?" God asked. "What about Nineveh? Shouldn't I have pity on its people?"

156
Israel Changes Forever
2 KINGS 17:1–41

Nineteen kings ruled Israel's ten tribes, and they all had nothing but trouble. Israel's kings did evil things and worshipped idols. Their army became weak, and the Assyrians captured the Israelites and stole everything they had. Nearly all the people were taken to faraway countries in the east. In these distant lands, the people of Israel changed forever. They married the foreign people and worshipped their gods. They forgot the real God, who had rescued them from Egypt long ago. This was the end of Israel's ten tribes. They never saw their own land again. God's ancient tribes became lost among the people of the Far East.

157
God's Law Is Taught in Judah
2 CHRONICLES 14:1–17:9

South of Israel was the kingdom of Judah. Its main city was Jerusalem, where Solomon's palace and his temple stood. Solomon's ancestors had been ruling the kingdom. His son and grandson had been its kings. They forgot about God, and this was bad for the kingdom.

When Solomon's great-grandson Asa became king, he loved God and tried to make things right by rebuilding the altar and destroying the statues of false gods. When Asa died, the people returned to their evil ways, but their new king, Jehoshaphat, would have none of it. He was Asa's son, and he loved God too! He destroyed the people's idols and sent his men throughout Judah to teach God's law.

158
King Jehoram
2 CHRONICLES 21:1–20

Judah's next king was Jehoshaphat's son, Jehoram. King Jehoram was married to Athaliah, one of Ahab and Jezebel's daughters, and soon he fell into their evil ways. Jehoram forgot about God, and he led his people away from God too. This all happened in Elijah's time.

Elijah sent a letter to King Jehoram:

God says, "You are not living
like your father and grandfather.
They were good kings.
You live like Ahab and his family.
They do evil things, and so do you.
The people in Judah have been led
away from Me because of you.
So I am going to bring trouble to you."

Enemy armies attacked Judah. They took everything that belonged to King Jehoram. Before long, the king got sick and died, but no one was sorry or even cared that their evil king was dead.

159
Joash, the Boy-King
2 CHRONICLES 22:1–23:21

After King Jehoram died, his son, Ahaziah, became Judah's king. Ahaziah's evil mother, Athaliah, knew her son's family was next in line for the throne, and this made her angry. *She* wanted to be queen! So Athaliah had her son and any heirs to the throne destroyed.

King Ahaziah's sister was married to a priest. She rescued the king's baby boy, Joash, and hid him in the temple.

Athaliah made herself queen and continued her evil ways. Then, one day, the priest brought the little boy out of hiding. Everyone knew he was the one who deserved to be king. The priest put a crown on Joash's head. The people shouted, "Long live the king!"

Queen Athaliah hurried to the temple to see what the shouting was about. "I've been tricked!" she cried.

"Take this woman out of the Lord's house," the priest commanded, and Queen Athaliah was dragged away.

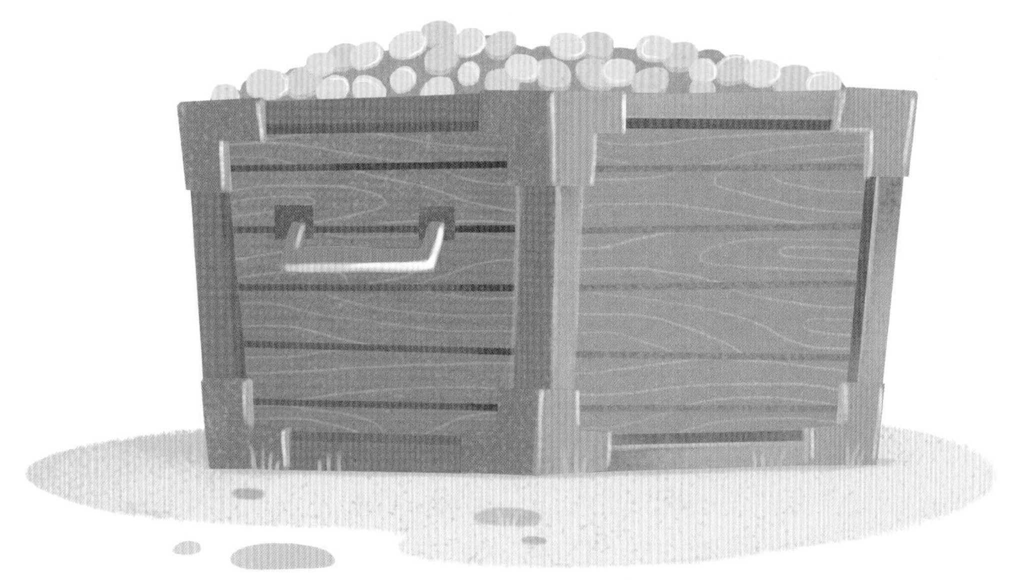

160
Joash Repairs the Temple
2 CHRONICLES 24:1–14

Joash, the boy-king, was just seven years old. He loved the Lord. When Joash became a man, he decided to repair Solomon's temple. It had been mistreated for many years. The temple was old and crumbling.

King Joash set a big box outside the temple doors. He asked everyone to bring gifts of money to the temple. The people were happy to do this. Day after day, the box was filled with money. The money was used to hire carpenters, metalworkers, and others. They all worked together to repair Solomon's temple—the Lord's house.

161
King Amaziah
2 CHRONICLES 24:23–25:28

Sadly, King Joash did what his ancestors had done. He left the Lord. The Syrians attacked Judah with their powerful army. King Joash died, and his son, Amaziah, became king.

Amaziah paid Israel silver in exchange for an army of one hundred thousand men. But a prophet told the king, "Don't bring their army with you. God isn't with them. Forget about your silver. God can give you much more than you lost."

King Amaziah didn't bring the army with him, but he brought idols—statues of false gods—and he worshipped them. "These gods can't save anyone," the prophet told him. "Why do you turn to them?" But Amaziah wouldn't listen.

Israel's army attacked Judah. They broke down Jerusalem's wall, robbed the temple, and then kidnapped the king.

162
King Uzziah
2 CHRONICLES 26:1–23

Amaziah's son, Uzziah, became Judah's next king. He was a good king, faithful to God, and his kingdom did well while he ruled. He loved fields, trees, and vineyards—the places where grapes grow—and his land produced good crops.

But, with power, Uzziah became proud. He decided he was above God's law. He thought he could do what priests did and go into the temple to offer incense. But Uzziah was not a priest. It was against the rules.

He went into the temple anyway, and the priests tried to send him away. "Leave here," they warned, "or there will be trouble for you." This made the king angry. He picked up the incense, and suddenly he had trouble. Uzziah's skin broke out with a terrible disease. The king ran from the temple, afraid because God had punished him.

His son, Jotham, became Judah's next king.

163
God's Prophet Isaiah
ISAIAH 6:1–9

The kings and their people continued to worship false gods and do other things that did not make God happy.

A man named Isaiah lived in the days of these kings. One day, Isaiah was worshipping in the temple when he saw God sitting on His throne surrounded by angels. The temple shook with voices: "Holy, holy, holy is the Lord of hosts."

Isaiah was afraid. He said, "I'm not perfect. I've said things that displease God, and now I see God!"

Suddenly, an angel brought a hot coal from a heavenly altar and touched Isaiah's lips with it. The angel said, "Your sin is taken away."

Then God spoke. "Who will be My messenger to the people?"

"Here I am, Lord," Isaiah answered. "Send me."

That day, God made Isaiah His prophet. "Go and speak to My people," God said.

164
"Speak My Words to the People"
ISAIAH 6:9–13

God said to Isaiah, "Go and speak My words to the people. They won't understand. My words will do them no good. They will close their ears and shut their eyes. They won't understand what you are telling them. They won't turn to Me and be healed from their evil ways."

Isaiah asked, "How long will this be, Lord?"

"Until no one lives in Judah's cities anymore," God said. "I will send everyone far away until their land is totally empty and nothing grows there. My people will be like an oak tree—cut to the ground. The stump is all that's left behind. Out of its roots, a new tree will grow."

Even though Isaiah's words seemed to do no good, God wanted him to continue speaking to His people. Sometime, far in the future, Judah's people would turn from their evil ways and serve God.

165
King Hezekiah
2 CHRONICLES 29:1–19

When King Hezekiah ruled, the first thing he did was order that God's temple be cleaned. He said to the priests, "Our ancestors have been untrue to God. They've done bad things and turned from Him. The temple—the Lord's house—has been forgotten. This is why God's anger came upon us. I want to make an agreement with God. I want Him to turn His anger away from us. So don't be lazy. God has chosen you to minister to Him and give Him offerings."

The priests went into the deepest part of the temple. There they found statues of idols. They burned them in Jerusalem's dump. The priests worked for more than two weeks and cleaned the Lord's house.

166
Hezekiah's Victory over Assyria
2 CHRONICLES 32:1–23

Hezekiah stayed close to God. When the Assyrian army invaded his kingdom, Hezekiah told the people, "Be strong. Don't be afraid. There is One who is greater than the strongest army. The Lord is here to help us and fight our battles."

The people strengthened Jerusalem's wall and were ready to fight. The Assyrians shouted to the people inside. They said terrible things about God and tried to persuade the people to turn from Him. Meanwhile, King Hezekiah and God's prophet Isaiah prayed.

God allowed the Assyrian commanders to be destroyed. The king and his army returned to their land. God saved Jerusalem from its enemies, and King Hezekiah became famous in all the nations.

167
The Sundial Moves Backward
2 KINGS 20:1–11

When King Hezekiah was old and sick, Assyria invaded Jerusalem again. The prophet Isaiah spoke to Hezekiah. "God says you will not get better. You will die soon."

Hezekiah prayed, "Remember, God, I've been faithful to You with my whole heart."

As Isaiah walked from the palace, God said, "Talk with Hezekiah again. Let him know that the God of his ancestor David has heard his prayer. Tell him I will heal him and add fifteen years to his life. The city will be saved from Assyria."

"How will the Lord prove that He will heal me?" Hezekiah asked.

"You choose," said Isaiah. "Shall the sundial [a tool that uses shadows to measure time] gain ten minutes or lose ten minutes?"

"It normally gains," said the king. "Let the shadow go backward."

Then Isaiah spoke to God, and the shadow moved backward by ten minutes. In three days, King Hezekiah was well.

168
King Manasseh
2 KINGS 21:1–18; 2 CHRONICLES 33:10–20

Manasseh, Hezekiah's son, became Judah's next king. He did evil things and led his people to do them too. They worshipped idols and brought statues of false gods back into the real God's temple. This made God very angry.

"Manasseh," God said, "you have been horrible. I'm going to bring much trouble to your kingdom. When people hear of it, their ears will tingle. My people have been causing Me anger since the day they left Egypt."

But Manasseh ignored God's words.

Then the Assyrian army captured King Manasseh. Manasseh prayed and cried to God for help. He knew only the one true God could save him. The Lord heard Manasseh's prayer and returned him to Jerusalem as king. Safe in Jerusalem, Manasseh destroyed the idols. He began the true worship of God and commanded his people to serve the Lord.

169
King Josiah
2 KINGS 22:1–23:20

King Manasseh's grandson, Josiah, was just eight years old when he became Judah's king. He followed the one true God. When he became a man, Josiah destroyed all the idols in Judah. No king had done that before. He even went outside Judah, breaking altars and burning images. Josiah crushed and burned the idol of the golden calf that King Jeroboam had set up two hundred years before.

Nearby, Josiah found a grave. "What is that grave marker I see?" he asked.

"This is the grave of the man of God from Judah," the people told him. "He came here when Jeroboam was king. This prophet predicted you would do what you're doing today."

"Let him rest," Josiah said. "No one should move his bones."

170
God's Lost Law Is Found
2 CHRONICLES 34:8–22

King Josiah destroyed the idols while others in his kingdom repaired the temple. Inside the temple, a priest found an old book written on rolls of leather. This was the book of the law that God had given to Moses many years before. It had been hidden so long that it was forgotten.

When King Josiah heard the words in the book read aloud, he said, "We've had all these troubles because our ancestors ignored God's Word." Then he sent the priest and some of his servants to Jerusalem, where Huldah the prophet lived. She would understand God's law.

171
Huldah Speaks God's Words
2 CHRONICLES 34:22–35:27

Huldah the prophet spoke for God: "Tell King Josiah that I am very angry with the people of Judah for leaving Me to worship false gods. My law says that Judah will have trouble. I will pour out My anger on this place. But King Josiah will die in peace before the trouble comes."

King Josiah called the priests, princes, and people to the temple. He read to them from the book of the law. Then they all promised to serve the Lord and keep His law. They kept this promise while Josiah was alive.

One day, the king and his army were fighting their enemy. Josiah died in the battle. The people in Judah were very sad. Josiah, the good king, had given them hope. Now a new king would be crowned, and no one knew what would happen next.

172
King Jehoiakim
2 KINGS 23:31–24:1; 2 CHRONICLES 36:1–7; JEREMIAH 36:1–25

Josiah's son Jehoahaz became Judah's new king. But the kingdom had a new pharaoh. He didn't like King Jehoahaz, so he captured him and put him in prison.

God's prophet Jeremiah told the people, "King Jehoahaz is never coming back."

Then Pharaoh made Jehoahaz's brother, Jehoiakim, king of Judah. He led the people back to worshipping idols and doing evil things.

God told Jeremiah to have someone write on a scroll all the things God had told him when Josiah was king. God said, "Maybe the people of Judah will hear what I am planning to do to them and will stop doing bad things."

Jeremiah's scroll was taken to King Jehoiakim. When the king heard God's words, he ignored them and burned the scroll. Then trouble came. Jerusalem was attacked by its enemies, and King Jehoiakim was killed.

173
Jeremiah Sees the Future
JEREMIAH 24:1–10

Babylon's King Nebuchadnezzar took control of Jerusalem and Judah. He captured their king and other important people and took them to Babylon.

God's prophet Jeremiah had a vision of the future. "What do you see, Jeremiah?" the Lord asked.

"Two baskets of figs. The good figs are very good. The bad ones are so bad they can't be eaten."

God explained, "The people who were captured and taken to Babylon are like the good figs. I'll care for them and bring them back to their land. They'll be My people, and I'll be their God. The bad figs are like the people left behind. I will allow them to have trouble for the rest of their lives."

Jeremiah wrote to those in Babylon: "You will, one day, return to your own land and have peace. God's thoughts are of peace and kindness toward you."

174
Jeremiah in a Muddy Pit
JEREMIAH 37:1–38:13

Nebuchadnezzar, King of Babylon, made a man named Zedekiah the next king of Judah. Zedekiah promised to serve King Nebuchadnezzar. But soon he broke that promise. Worried, Zedekiah prayed to his false gods for help. But nothing changed.

Jeremiah warned Zedekiah, "You're going to be handed over to Nebuchadnezzar, Babylon's king. The people who go with the Babylonians will live. Those who stay to fight will not."

Jeremiah's words made the king so angry that he threw Jeremiah into a muddy pit and left him to die. But an Ethiopian man rescued Jeremiah. He used ropes to pull him out of the pit.

175
Jerusalem Is Destroyed
2 CHRONICLES 36:15–21; JEREMIAH 39:1–10

Nebuchadnezzar's army surrounded Jerusalem. The people there were trapped, starving, and sick. The Babylonians broke through Jerusalem's city wall. Soldiers burned the temple and the houses, and the people who remained were made Nebuchadnezzar's servants. All the treasures in Jerusalem's palace and the temple were brought out, and King Nebuchadnezzar took them to Babylon. Four hundred years had passed since Judah's first king, Rehoboam, ruled. Now God's people were slaves again. Jerusalem, the City of David, was torn apart, and Solomon's temple was a heap of ashes.

176
Songs in a Strange Land
PSALM 137:1–6

The captives in Babylon didn't forget their homeland. Their children learned songs about their history. Though they were often sad, they sang.

We sat down and cried by the rivers of Babylon
when we remembered the hills in Jerusalem.
There upon the trees we played our harps.
Our enemies there made us sing.
Those who made it hard for us asked us to entertain them.
They said, "Sing to us one of the songs of your land."

How can we sing the song of the Lord in a strange land?
If I forget you, O Jerusalem, may my right hand forget what it is able to do.
May my tongue hold to the roof of my mouth if I do not remember you.
I will remember Jerusalem with the greatest joy.

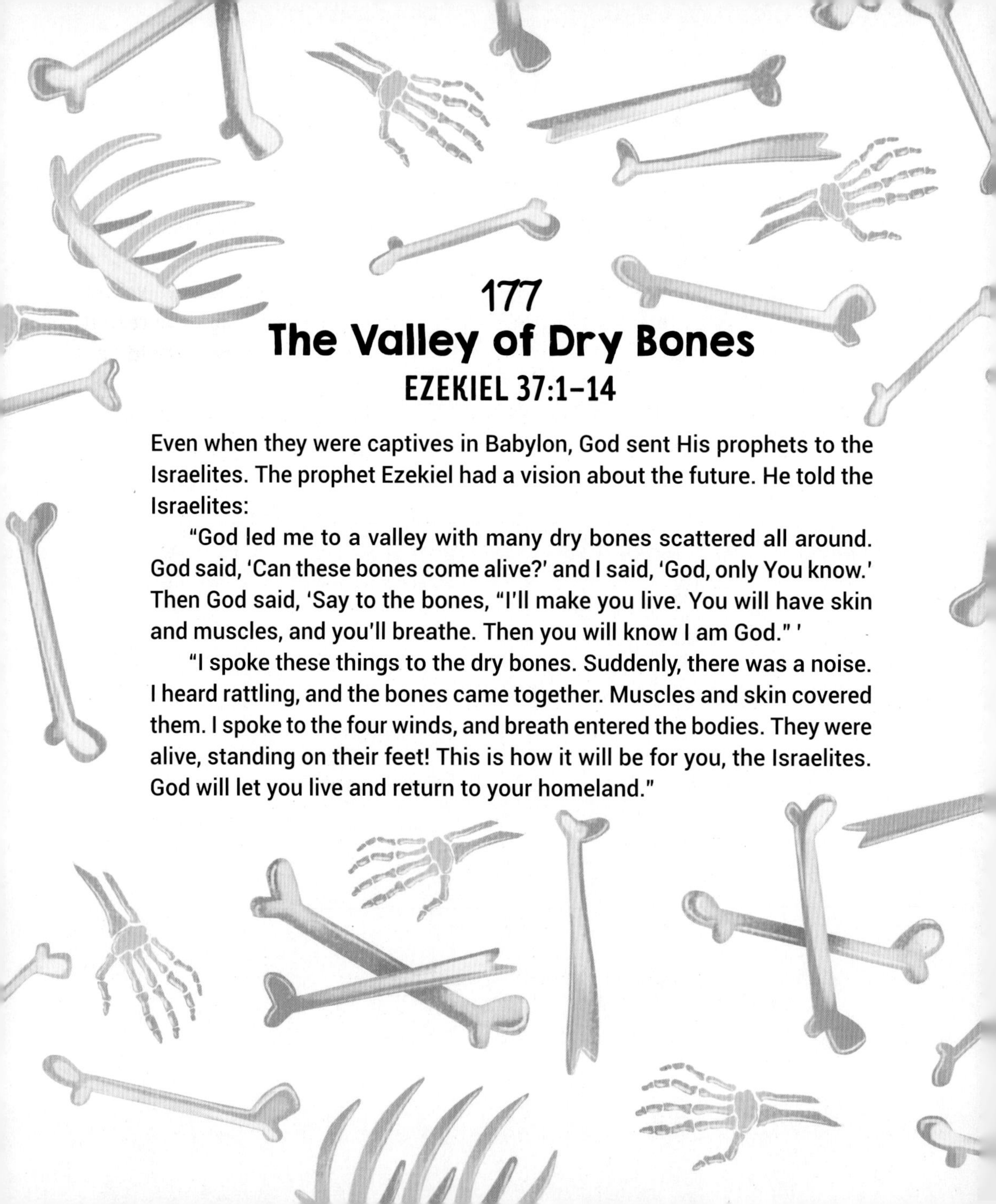

177

The Valley of Dry Bones

EZEKIEL 37:1–14

Even when they were captives in Babylon, God sent His prophets to the Israelites. The prophet Ezekiel had a vision about the future. He told the Israelites:

"God led me to a valley with many dry bones scattered all around. God said, 'Can these bones come alive?' and I said, 'God, only You know.' Then God said, 'Say to the bones, "I'll make you live. You will have skin and muscles, and you'll breathe. Then you will know I am God." '

"I spoke these things to the dry bones. Suddenly, there was a noise. I heard rattling, and the bones came together. Muscles and skin covered them. I spoke to the four winds, and breath entered the bodies. They were alive, standing on their feet! This is how it will be for you, the Israelites. God will let you live and return to your homeland."

178
Daniel and His Friends
DANIEL 1:1–7

Among the captives in Babylon was a young man named Daniel. God planned for him to become a great prophet.

King Nebuchadnezzar wanted young Israelites to serve in his palace. He wanted smart, handsome, strong men. Each had to learn the Babylonian language and read its books. The king's wise men would teach them for three years. Then they would have jobs in the royal palace.

Along with Daniel, there were Hananiah, Mishael, and Azariah. These men were all from Judah. The king ordered that they be given Babylonian names. Daniel was called Belteshazzar, and the others were called Shadrach, Meshach, and Abednego.

179
Daniel's Wisdom
DANIEL 1:8–21

While being taught by the wise men at the king's palace, Daniel and his friends were given food that had been offerings to false gods. Daniel knew the real God would not be happy if he ate it. The palace master said, "The king has given you this food to make you strong and healthy. If you don't eat it, the king will be angry with me."

Daniel suggested, "For ten days, give us just vegetables and water. Then see if we're healthy." The palace master agreed. After ten days, Daniel and his three friends looked healthier than the others.

God made Daniel and his friends wise. They learned all about the Babylonians. Daniel could also understand dreams and visions. Daniel and his friends knew far more than the king's own wise men. King Nebuchadnezzar was pleased. Daniel and his friends became part of the king's court, and the king trusted them.

180
Daniel's Good Judgment
DANIEL 2:1–24

King Nebuchadnezzar had a troubling dream. "I must know what it means," he said.

"Tell us your dream, O king," said his wise men. "We'll tell you its meaning."

"If you are so wise, then tell me not only what my dream means but also what I dreamed," said the king.

"No one on earth can know what you dreamed," his wise men answered.

The king flew into a rage. "Destroy all the wise men in Babylon!" he shouted. (This meant Daniel and his friends too.)

Daniel used his wisdom to keep himself from harm. So the king allowed the men more time. Then Daniel and his friends prayed, asking God to save their lives. That night God gave Daniel the meaning of the king's dream.

"Take me to the king," said Daniel. "I'll tell him what he dreamed and its meaning."

181
The King's Dream
DANIEL 2:27–49

"Nobody on earth can tell your dream's meaning," Daniel told King Nebuchadnezzar. "But my God can. You saw a huge, shining statue. Its head was gold, its chest and arms silver, its middle bronze. Its legs, iron. Its feet, iron and clay. You saw a stone being cut out. It fell and broke the statue's feet. Then the entire statue fell, and its pieces blew away. The stone became a great mountain, filling the earth.

"Your kingdom is the gold head. Another kingdom will come—the statue's silver shoulders and arms. Then a third kingdom of bronze. A kingdom strong as iron will rise. Finally, a divided kingdom that is partly strong will rule. In those days, God will set up His forever kingdom. It will end all the earth's kingdoms and grow to fill the whole earth."

Nebuchadnezzar cried in disbelief, "Your God is the God of all gods!"

182
Shadrach, Meshach, and Abednego
DANIEL 3:1–23

Nebuchadnezzar had a giant golden statue made. It was ninety feet tall. He commanded his kingdom to worship the statue or be thrown into a fiery furnace. Everyone worshipped the idol Nebuchadnezzar set up—everyone except Daniel's friends, Shadrach, Meshach, and Abednego. They stood before the angry king.

"You must worship the golden statue I've made. If not, you'll be thrown into the furnace," the king said.

"Nebuchadnezzar, we can only say this: we believe our God can save us from the furnace. If He doesn't, we still won't serve your gods, nor will we worship your golden statue."

Nebuchadnezzar's face became red with anger. "Heat the furnace seven times hotter than ever before," he commanded. Then his strongest guards tied up Shadrach, Meshach, and Abednego. The furnace raged with heat, and the three men were thrown inside.

183

Four Men Walk in the Fire

DANIEL 3:24–30

When King Nebuchadnezzar looked into the furnace, he asked his servants, "Didn't you put three men inside?"

"We did!" they promised.

"But I see four men, untied, walking through the fire. They aren't hurt at all. One of them looks like a god." Then the king called, "Shadrach, Meshach, Abednego, servants of the Most High God, come out!"

Shadrach, Meshach, and Abednego climbed out of the furnace. They were perfectly fine, and their clothing didn't even smell like fire and smoke.

"The God of Shadrach, Meshach, and Abednego is powerful and real. No other god could do this," the king said. Then he commanded his people: "No one may ever speak against their God."

184
God's Lesson to Nebuchadnezzar Part One
DANIEL 4:1–18

King Nebuchadnezzar had another strange dream. His wise men couldn't tell the king what it meant, so the king called for Daniel.

"There was a very strong, tall tree," the king said. "Its top reached to heaven. Everyone on earth could see its beautiful leaves and fruit. This tree gave food to all the people. Animals rested in its shade, and birds nested in its branches. Then I saw an angel who said, 'Cut down the tree and chop off its branches. Strip off its leaves and scatter its fruit. Let the animals run and fly away from it. Leave the tree's stump and its roots in the ground. For seven years, the stump will have the mind of an animal. Then everyone will know that God rules over the earth.'

"Now, Daniel. Tell me what it means."

185
God's Lesson to Nebuchadnezzar Part Two
DANIEL 4:19–37

"The tall, strong tree is you, King," said Daniel. "You've grown great and strong. Your greatness reaches to heaven, and your power covers the earth.

"The angel's words are from God. You, King Nebuchadnezzar, will be driven away from everyone and live with wild animals. Seven years will pass. The stump means your kingdom will return. This will happen when you learn that God is all-powerful. Take my advice, King. Leave your sins, and care for others. Then God will give you more days of peace."

Everything in the dream did happen to Nebuchadnezzar. He was sent away. He ate grass like an ox. His hair grew long like eagles' feathers. His fingernails were like birds' claws. After seven years, the king turned to God and honored Him. Then Nebuchadnezzar became king again—and with God's help, he was even greater and more powerful than before.

186

The Handwriting on the Wall Part One

DANIEL 5:1–12

Years passed, and King Nebuchadnezzar's descendant Belshazzar had become king of Babylon. He had a great feast where the guests praised and honored their false gods. "Bring the gold and silver cups from Solomon's temple," Belshazzar commanded. Then all the people drank from the cups that had been stolen from the Holy Place in Jerusalem.

Suddenly, a hand appeared! It began writing strange words on the palace wall. The king was terrified. "Bring my wise men to read the words!" he demanded.

The wise men came, but they could not understand what the hand had written.

The king's mother had been watching and listening. "There's a certain man in your kingdom who is very wise," she said. "He can even explain dreams. His name is Daniel. Let him come to read the words."

187
The Handwriting on the Wall Part Two
DANIEL 5:13–31

Daniel was old now. He told King Belshazzar, "I was here when God gave your ancestor Nebuchadnezzar this kingdom. But Nebuchadnezzar became proud and was sent away. When he turned to God, he returned and became great again. You are also proud. You drank from cups stolen from God's house. You haven't praised God who gives you power. So God sent this hand to write on your wall.

"The words are MENE TEKEL UPHARSIN. *Mene* means numbered; *tekel* means weighed; *upharsin* means divided. The days of your kingdom are numbered. Your weight—your power—is light. Your kingdom is divided. It's been given to your enemies, the Persians."

After Daniel spoke, that very night the Persians invaded Babylon, and Belshazzar was no longer the king.

188
A New King and a New Law
DANIEL 6:1–10

The Persians declared Darius the new king of Babylon.

King Darius made Daniel one of three officials in his kingdom. Daniel was the king's favorite, and the other two were jealous of Daniel. They decided to cause him big trouble.

They knew Daniel prayed to the one true God three times a day. So they went to the king and said, "O king, everyone should pray to you and not to any other god. We want you to make a new law: everyone must bow down and worship you. If they do not, they will be thrown to the lions."

The king agreed. But Daniel would not turn from his God. He continued to pray to God three times a day.

189
Daniel in the Lions' Den
DANIEL 6:11–17

When the officials saw Daniel praying, they went to the king. "There is someone, O king, who doesn't obey your law. It is Daniel. Before the law, he prayed to his God three times a day. And he still does."

This news upset King Darius. He didn't want Daniel thrown to the lions. He spent the whole day trying to decide how to save him. Still, that evening, the jealous officials insisted that Daniel be punished.

Darius had to honor his law. Daniel was brought and put into a cave with the lions. "You've served your God faithfully, Daniel," the king said. "I hope your God will save you." A stone was brought to seal the mouth of the cave. No one could let Daniel out of the lions' den.

190
God Saves Daniel
DANIEL 6:18–28

King Darius couldn't sleep because he was so worried about Daniel in the den with those hungry lions. Early the next morning, the king hurried to the lions' den and called out, "Daniel, has your God kept you safe from the lions?" The king thought he would hear the lions' roars. Instead, he heard Daniel say, "God sent His angel to save me. The angel shut the lions' mouths. God knew I had done nothing wrong. The lions haven't harmed me."

The king had Daniel taken out of the den. Then he punished the two officials who were so jealous of Daniel.

191
The Israelites Return to Jerusalem
EZRA 1:1–2:67

Years before, God's prophet Jeremiah had said that the Israelites would someday be captured by the Babylonians. He said they would remain slaves for seventy years.

When seventy years passed, Cyrus was Babylon's king. He said, "The Lord has given me all the kingdoms on earth. He has told me to build His temple at Jerusalem. All God's people have my permission to go there. They may rebuild the house of the Lord. God be with them! Give them silver and gold, goods, and animals to make offerings at the temple."

More than forty thousand Jews returned to Jerusalem. They brought precious offerings for the temple. Thousands of servants and two hundred singers went with them. They traveled in a caravan with horses, mules, camels, and donkeys.

192
The Rebuilding Begins
EZRA 2:70–3:13

When the Jews returned to Jerusalem, they found the city in ruins. Before long, they began rebuilding God's temple. They found the place of the first altar where, many years before, Abraham had offered Isaac to God. This was the same place Solomon had built his temple.

Builders cleared the space and laid the building's foundation. The priests were there with trumpets. Others had cymbals. They sang this song to the Lord: "For He is good, for His steady love lasts forever toward Israel."

All the people praised the Lord. Many were old people. They'd seen the first temple at this place. The people cried tears of joy. They shouted with joy! The sound of weeping and shouting was heard far away.

193

The Enemies

EZRA 4:1–16

The Samaritans lived north of Jerusalem. Some worshipped the one true God, but others worshipped false gods. They wanted to help rebuild the temple, but one of the priests, Zerubbabel, said no. "King Cyrus commanded that *we* rebuild it," he said.

This made the Samaritans angry. They tried to stop the work. A new king had come into power in Babylon, which was now called Persia. His name was Artaxerxes. The Samaritans sent him a letter:

The Jews have come to Jerusalem. They're rebuilding that wicked city and its walls. If the city is built, the Jews won't pay your taxes. We're true to you and don't want you put to shame. History shows that Jerusalem was destroyed because of its enemies. If it's rebuilt, you'll lose your power on this side of the river.

194
The Prophets
EZRA 4:17–5:2

Artaxerxes replied to the enemies of those rebuilding God's temple—

To the Samaritan leaders:

I find that Jerusalem has had mighty kings. They ruled the country beyond the river. Jerusalem made war against the kings of past empires. These people must stop their work at Jerusalem. The city cannot be rebuilt until I decide it can.

The Samaritans had won. They forced the building to stop. But, before long, there was a new king in Persia called Darius. At the same time, two prophets named Haggai and Zechariah came to Jerusalem.

"God's house is in ruins," the prophet Haggai scolded the Jews. "Build the house. Its glory will be greater than that of Solomon's temple."

Zechariah spoke God's words: " 'My house isn't built by power, but by My spirit,' says the Lord. 'The priest Zerubbabel laid the temple's foundation. His hands will finish it.' "

So the Jews continued rebuilding the temple.

195
The King's Command
EZRA 5:11–6:12

The Jerusalem leaders wrote to King Darius:

Many years ago, our ancestors made God angry. So King Nebuchadnezzar destroyed God's temple, captured the Israelites, and made them slaves in Babylon. All the temple's holy things were taken there. We are rebuilding God's temple. Please search your records. Read the command of King Cyrus for the rebuilding. Then write to us your decision.

The king found a scroll with Cyrus's orders to rebuild God's temple. He sent his decision to Jerusalem:

Continue rebuilding. The Samaritans will give their taxes to pay for the building and give the priests everything they need for their gifts to God. This is my command.

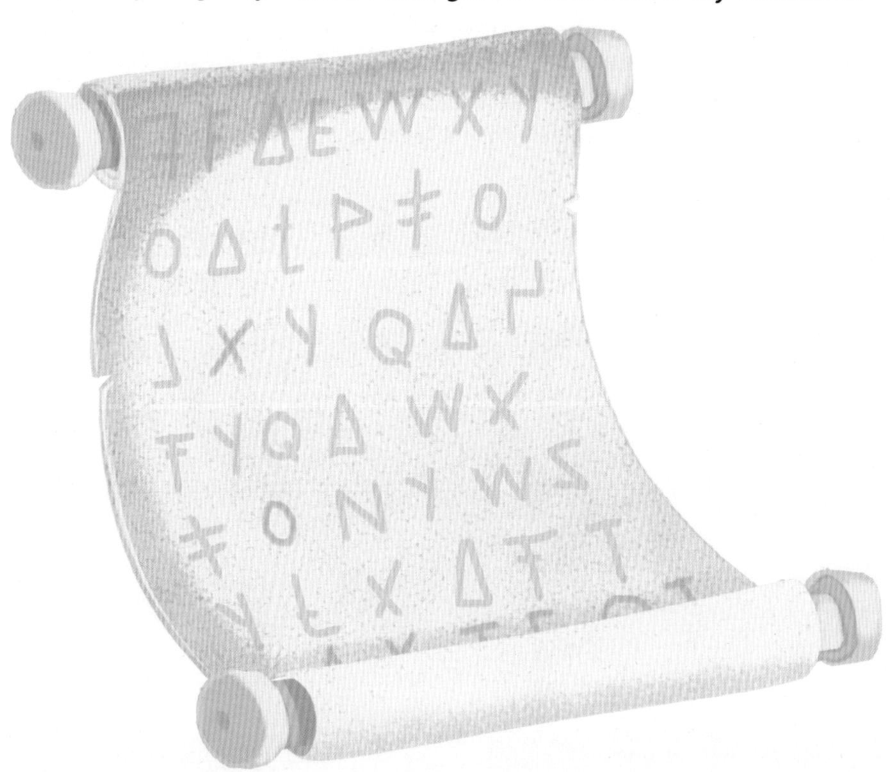

196
The Temple Is Finished
EZRA 6:13–22

With the help of God's words from the prophets Haggai and Zechariah, the Jews rebuilt the temple. When the temple was finished, there was a huge and happy celebration. The people brought many offerings to God, and they celebrated the anniversary of the Passover that had happened many years before. The celebration went on for seven days.

The second temple was much like the one Solomon had built, but one thing was missing—the ark of the covenant had been lost and not returned to Jerusalem.

197
An Empire with No Queen
ESTHER 1:1–2:4

After King Darius died, his son, Ahasuerus, became the next king. His wife, Vashti, was queen. At a huge banquet, Ahasuerus wanted everyone to see his beautiful queen, but Vashti refused to come to the party. This made the king very angry. "What shall I do with Vashti?" he asked his counselors.

"Never see her again," they said. "Choose another queen."

So Ahasuerus sent letters throughout the Persian empire, declaring that Vashti was no longer his queen.

His counselors suggested, "Bring women from all over the empire. Choose a new queen from among them."

So young women from everywhere were brought to the king's palace.

198
Queen Esther
ESTHER 2:5–23

Mordecai and his cousin, a beautiful young woman named Esther, were Jews who hadn't returned to Jerusalem. They lived in King Ahasuerus's empire. Mordecai had been like a father to Esther after her parents died.

Esther was among the women brought to Ahasuerus's palace. Mordecai told Esther to keep it secret that she was a Jew. He worried that if the king found out, Esther might be in danger.

In time, King Ahasuerus chose Esther over all the other women and made her his queen. When he wanted to see Esther, he sent for her. No one could go to the king's rooms without an invitation—not even the queen.

One day, Mordecai was sitting by the palace gate when he overheard two men planning to kill King Ahasuerus. Mordecai sent a message to Esther, who told the king. The men were captured and punished. Mordecai had saved the king's life.

199
Haman's Plan
ESTHER 3:1–6

King Ahasuerus gave a man named Haman power in the empire. The king allowed Haman to do whatever he wanted. The king even commanded that people bow to Haman whenever he passed by. Everyone bowed to him except Mordecai, who only bowed to worship God.

Haman was very angry that Mordecai wouldn't bow to him. So he decided to punish not just Mordecai, but all the Jews living in Persia.

No one knew—not even Haman or the king—that Queen Esther was Mordecai's cousin and that she was a Jew.

200
Haman Plots against the Jews
ESTHER 3:7–4:8

Haman told the king, "Some people in your kingdom don't obey your laws. You should command that they all be destroyed."

"Do whatever seems best to you," the king replied. So Haman wrote orders to every part of the king's empire:

On the thirteenth day of the twelfth month, wipe out all the Jews and take their property.

He marked the orders with the king's stamp.

When Mordecai heard of the law, he went to the king's gate. Mordecai gave the queen's servant a copy of the order with a message. "Take this to Esther," he said.

201
"If I Die, I Die"
ESTHER 4:9–5:8

Mordecai's message said: "Esther, beg the king to save your people."

Esther replied, "No one can go to the king's rooms without an invitation or they'll die."

Mordecai responded, "You'll be destroyed with all the Jews. You may be silent, Esther, but God will rescue us another way. Who knows? Maybe you've become queen for just this reason."

"Gather the Jews to pray," Esther told him. "Pray for three days. Then I'll go to the king. If I die, I die."

After three days, Esther went to the king. "What do you wish, Esther?" he asked. "I'll give you anything."

"I've come to ask you and Haman to dinner," she said.

The king granted her wish. Esther, the king, and Haman ate together. Then the king asked, "What do you wish, Esther?"

"Let's all have dinner again tomorrow," she answered. "Then I will tell you."

202
The King Honors Mordecai
ESTHER 5:9–6:11

Haman went home and told his wife, "I dined with the king, and yet Mordecai refuses to bow to someone as important as me."

"So destroy him," Haman's wife said.

That night, King Ahasuerus couldn't sleep, so he read the history of his empire. There he learned that Mordecai had saved his life. *I wonder how I can honor this man,* he thought.

The next day, the king asked Haman, "What is the best way for me to honor a man?"

Haman thought the king meant him. "Give the man your best robes and your horse. Send a nobleman with him as he rides through the city. The nobleman should shout, 'This is the man the king honors!' "

"Quickly, do this for Mordecai, the Jew," ordered the king. Then he sent Haman to be the nobleman to shout, "Mordecai is the man the king honors!"

203

"The Wicked Haman!"

ESTHER 7:1-6

The king, Haman, and Esther had dinner together again. "What do you wish for, Esther?" asked the king. "I'll give you anything, even half my kingdom."

"Let my life be spared," Esther answered. "And don't wipe out my people, the Jews. There's an evil plot against us. It will not be good for your empire."

King Ahasuerus said to Queen Esther, "Who is the one who made this plan? Where is he who has imagined this thing?"

"He is this man—the wicked Haman!" said the queen.

204
The Jews Celebrate
ESTHER 7:7–10:3

King Ahasuerus was so angry! Haman begged the queen for mercy, but the king's guards hauled him away. Then the king gave Esther everything that had belonged to the wicked man.

Esther told the king her secret—that Mordecai was her cousin. "O king," said Esther, "cancel the order to destroy my people."

The king gave Mordecai a ring that had been on Haman's finger. Then he said, "Write an order. Say what you please. Put my stamp on it." So Mordecai wrote the order commanding that the Jewish people be saved.

A special festival, a celebration called Purim, was ordered by Queen Esther. To this day, Jews celebrate Purim. They tell the story of Esther and Mordecai.

205
Ezra Returns to Jerusalem
EZRA 7:1–10:44

The Jews had been living in Judea for ninety years. Jerusalem was a small town with ruined houses and no city wall. Often, its people were robbed by bandits.

Ezra was a Jewish priest living in Babylon. He studied God's law and taught it to others. Ezra gathered the ancient writings and wrote them down on scrolls. For the first time, the Old Testament books were all together. Ezra took them to Jerusalem.

There, Ezra found Jews who had married foreigners. They worshipped idols and hadn't taught their children about the real God and His law. Ezra prayed, crying out to God, "We are only the leftovers of Your people, the Israelites. Our guilt has piled up to heaven. We cannot face You because of this." Then Ezra sent away everyone who had married a foreigner. They left Jerusalem with their wives and children.

206
Nehemiah Goes to Jerusalem
NEHEMIAH 1:1–2:9

Nehemiah lived in Persia and served its king, but he loved Jerusalem. When men from Judea came visiting, Nehemiah asked, "How is the city?"

When he heard Jerusalem was in ruins with no city wall, Nehemiah cried and prayed, "O God, hear my prayer. You promised to gather the Israelites to Jerusalem from under the farthest skies. You rescued them with Your great power. I will speak to the king about this. Cause him to grant my request."

Nehemiah went to the king and breathed a silent prayer. "The city where my ancestors are buried is in ruins," he said.

"What is it you want?" asked the king.

"Send me to Jerusalem where my ancestors are. Let me rebuild the city," Nehemiah said.

So the king released Nehemiah from his service and let him go.

207
Nehemiah–The Builder
NEHEMIAH 2:11–3:32

Nehemiah traveled to Jerusalem. Later, he wrote down what happened there:

I got up in the night. A few men and I went to look at Jerusalem's wall. It was in ruins, and the gates were burned to ash. Then I said to its people, "Come, let us rebuild the wall of Jerusalem. Then people will respect us again." I told them the king had sent me.

"Let's start building!" they agreed.

People in the nearby lands mocked us, but I told them, "The God of heaven will give us success. The Jews are going to start building, and you cannot share in this work."

Each family in Jerusalem agreed to build part of the wall. The high priest built one of the gates. A rich man built a long section. Others did a little. Some built much. Some built nothing.

208
The Wall Is Finished
NEHEMIAH 4:1–6:16

When the people started building the city wall, their enemies mocked them. But as the Jews built Jerusalem's wall higher, their enemies—the Arabians, the Ammonites, and the Ashdodites—were angry. They didn't want Jerusalem to be strong.

The Jews guarded the wall day and night while the work continued.

"Don't be afraid of them," said Nehemiah. "Remember, the Lord is great and awesome."

When their enemies saw they couldn't attack, they sent a message to Nehemiah, inviting him to meet them in a nearby valley. They plotted to attack him there. But Nehemiah outsmarted them. "I'm doing a great work," he said. "Why should this work stop while I meet with you?"

After fifty-two days, the wall was finished. The gates were closed, and guards stood around. Jerusalem's enemies were afraid. They knew the work had been done with God's help.

209

Ezra Reads the Law

NEHEMIAH 8:1–13:31

The Jews gathered at the gate and said to Ezra, "Bring us the law of Moses." Ezra brought the scrolls. He blessed the Lord, and all the people answered, "Amen. Amen." From early morning until noon, Ezra read to them. "This day is holy to the Lord," Ezra and the priests told them. Then the people returned to their homes to a joyful feast.

When Nehemiah returned to Jerusalem, he saw its people working on the Sabbath. "This is against God's law for the Jews. What is this evil thing you're doing?" Nehemiah asked. "How can you dishonor the Sabbath?" Then he ordered that the city gates be closed at sunset before the Sabbath and not opened until the morning after the Sabbath.

Jerusalem began to grow and get better as Jews returned there from all lands.

210
Zechariah Sees an Angel
LUKE 1:5–23

Years passed, and now King Herod ruled Judea. At the temple was a priest named Zechariah. His wife was Elizabeth.

One day, Zechariah was at the temple when he saw an angel. Zechariah was terrified!

"Fear not," the angel said. "God has heard your prayers. Elizabeth will have a baby boy. You'll name him John. People will rejoice when he's born. He'll have Elijah's spirit and turn many to the Lord."

"How do I know this is true?" Zechariah asked. "I'm an old man, and Elizabeth is too old to have a baby."

"I'm Gabriel," said the angel. "God sent me to give you good news. But because you don't believe me, you won't be able to speak until your son is born."

When Zechariah came out of the temple, he tried to use his hands to tell the people what had happened, but they couldn't understand.

211
Gabriel Visits Mary
LUKE 1:24–38

When Elizabeth heard she and Zechariah would have a baby, she was very happy. "This is what God has done for me!" she said.

Next, God's angel Gabriel went to a town called Nazareth—a place in Galilee north of Judea. Elizabeth's cousin Mary lived there. She was engaged to a man named Joseph. "Greetings, Mary," Gabriel said. "You are favored by God. He is with you."

Mary was confused. "What do you mean?" she asked.

"Don't be afraid," Gabriel told her. "You are going to have a baby boy. You will name Him Jesus. He will be called the Son of God."

212
John the Baptist Is Born
LUKE 1:39–80

"Hello, Elizabeth!" Mary had come to see her cousin.

When Elizabeth heard Mary's voice, her baby jumped inside her belly. "Mary! You are the most blessed of all women," Elizabeth exclaimed. "When I heard your voice, my baby jumped for joy inside me."

Several months after their visit, Elizabeth's son, John, was born. He would one day grow up to be a priest for God and a prophet. John would live in the wilderness and become known as John the Baptist.

213
Jesus Christ Is Born!
MATTHEW 1:18–21; LUKE 2:1–7

Mary's husband-to-be, Joseph, was a carpenter in Nazareth. In his dreams, an angel spoke to Joseph: "Take Mary as your wife. The child in her is from God's Holy Spirit. When the baby is born, call Him Jesus. He will save God's people from their sins."

In those days, Emperor Augustus Caesar commanded that everyone in his kingdom be counted. This meant they had to return to their hometowns. Mary and Joseph made the long, hard journey to Bethlehem. When they arrived, they found no rooms at the inn—the place where visitors stayed. So Mary and Joseph went to a stable where animals lived. There, Mary had her baby. They named Him Jesus. Mary wrapped Him in a blanket and made a bed for Him in the hay in a manger—a long box animals eat from.

214

"I've Come to Give You Good News!"

LUKE 2:8–20

That night, shepherds watched over their sheep in the fields near Bethlehem. Suddenly, a great, bright light surrounded them. An angel appeared, and the shepherds were terrified.

"Don't be afraid," the angel told them. "I've come to give you good news. Today, in Bethlehem, Christ the Lord has been born. You'll find Him wrapped in a blanket, sleeping in a manger." Then the sky became filled with angels praising God, saying: "Glory to God in heaven! On earth, peace and goodwill."

"Let's go to Bethlehem and see this wonderful thing," said the shepherds.

When they got to the stable, they found Mary, Joseph, and the baby Jesus, who was sleeping in the manger just as the angel had said.

215

Simeon's Praise

LUKE 2:21–35

One day, Mary and Joseph brought their baby to the temple. Jewish law said they needed to promise Him to God. An old man named Simeon was led by God's Holy Spirit to go to the temple too. When he saw Mary, Joseph, and the baby, he said, "Many in Israel will rise and fall because of your child." Then Simeon held Jesus in his arms and praised God. "Thank You, Lord, for letting me leave this life in peace," he said. "I've finally seen Your salvation for all people. Jesus will be a light so the Gentiles can see You; and He will be the glory of Your people, Israel."

216
The Star
MATTHEW 2:1–10

Far from Bethlehem, in the East, lived wise men who studied the stars. When they saw a bright, unusual star, they followed it. The men traveled to Jerusalem and began asking people, "Where is the child who is born to be King of the Jews? We saw His star in the sky, so we came to honor Him."

This worried King Herod. A prophet named Micah had said long ago that the ruler of Israel would come out of the little town of Bethlehem. If that was Jesus, the Christ, Herod was afraid he might lose his kingdom. Herod didn't know where Jesus was. So he said to the wise men, "When you've found the child, tell me. I want to honor Him too." But this was a lie.

The wise men followed the star to Bethlehem until they found it stopped there, shining brightly over a house.

217
Gifts for the Christ Child
MATTHEW 2:11–14

The wise men were happy that they found Jesus. Inside the house, they saw Mary with the child. They kneeled before Him. Then, opening their treasure chests, they offered Jesus gifts. They gave Him precious gold and special herbs called frankincense and myrrh.

When the men left, they didn't return to Herod and tell him where Jesus was. In a dream, one of them had been warned not to do this. So they traveled back to their land by another road.

Joseph had been warned in a dream too. An angel told him, "Take Mary and Jesus to Egypt. King Herod wants to destroy the child!"

So that very night, the family left Bethlehem for Egypt, where they would be safe.

218
Jesus in Egypt
MATTHEW 2:15–23

Herod was angry that the wise men hadn't told him where Jesus was. So he ordered that all baby boys in Bethlehem be destroyed. That way, he would be sure to do away with Jesus, King of the Jews.

But the little boy, Jesus, was safe in Egypt with His family. Years later, after Herod died, an angel came to Joseph in a dream and told him, "Get up and go back to Israel." Herod's son was ruling in Judea, so instead of going there, Joseph took his family to Nazareth in Galilee where they would be safe.

All this happened according to God's plan and had been talked about many years before by God's prophets.

219

In His Father's House

LUKE 2:40–52

When Jesus was twelve years old, His family went to Jerusalem to celebrate the Passover. Afterward, when His family was on their way home, they realized Jesus wasn't with them. So they went back to Jerusalem to look for Him. Three days later, they found Jesus with those who taught God's law in the temple. The teachers were amazed at how much Jesus knew and what He said.

"We have been looking for You!" Jesus' mother said. "We've been worried sick."

"Why were you searching for Me?" Jesus asked her. "Didn't you know I would be in My Father's house?" But Mary didn't understand what Jesus meant.

Jesus returned to Nazareth with His family, and He obeyed His parents. His mother always remembered the things He did and said at the temple.

As Jesus grew older, He also grew in wisdom, and God was pleased with Him.

220

John the Baptist

MATTHEW 3:1–6; LUKE 3:1–6

Years passed, and Jesus and his cousin John were both young men. John lived in the wilderness. He wore a leather belt and clothing made from camel hair. He ate dried grasshoppers and wild honey from the trees. When John was thirty years old, God sent him to the Jewish people. He told them to turn from sin—the bad things people do—and God would forgive them. In the Jordan River, John baptized people who turned away from sin. He said: "Turn from sin and do right. The kingdom of heaven is nearby. Its King will soon be here." He meant Jesus, but the people didn't understand.

All this happened according to God's plan and had been talked about many years before by God's prophets.

221
John Baptizes Jesus
MATTHEW 3:13–17; LUKE 3:15–22

People wondered if John the Baptist was the Christ—the One that God had promised to send to save them from sin. They knew John was close to God and spoke God's words. But John told them, "I baptize you with water. The One who is coming is greater than I am. He will baptize you with the Holy Spirit and fire." John was speaking of Jesus.

One day, Jesus came to the river to be baptized by John. "You should baptize me!" John told Him.

"It is right for us to do this," Jesus answered. So John baptized Jesus.

Just then, God's Spirit came down like a dove, and God spoke: "This is My Son, whom I love. He makes Me happy."

222
Jesus and the Devil
LUKE 4:1–13

God's Spirit led Jesus into the wilderness. There, God allowed Satan—the devil—to try to convince Jesus to do something that God would not like. But Jesus wouldn't do it.

When Jesus was hungry, Satan said, "If You are God's Son, make these stones into bread."

Jesus answered, "One doesn't only live on bread. God's words are food as well."

Then Satan took Him to the temple roof. "The angels won't let You get hurt," he said. "So jump to the ground."

"It is written, 'Don't put God to the test,' " Jesus told him.

Then Satan said, "I'll give You all of earth's kingdoms. Worship me!"

But Jesus replied, "Get away, Satan! The Bible says, 'Worship and serve only God.' "

The devil left Him, and then angels came and cared for Jesus.

223
Jesus' Followers
JOHN 1:29–51

Jesus went to the Jordan River. When John saw Him, he said, "Look! It's the One who takes away the world's sin. This is the One I said was greater than I am. I've seen this, and now I tell you: this is the Son of God!"

Two of John's followers heard what John said, and they started to walk behind Jesus.

Jesus turned around. "What are you looking for?" He asked.

"Teacher," they replied, "where are You going?"

"Come and see."

One man, Andrew, found his brother, Simon, and said, "We've found the Christ!"

He brought Simon to Jesus, and Jesus said to Simon, "You are called Simon. But I'm giving you a new name—Peter."

They all walked to Galilee, where they found Philip. "Follow Me," Jesus said.

They met a man named Nathaniel. "Teacher," Nathaniel said, "You are the Son of God! You are the King of Israel!"

224

"You Will Fish for People"

MATTHEW 4:18–22

Peter and Andrew earned money catching and selling fish. Jesus watched as they cast their nets into the Sea of Galilee. He said to them, "Follow Me, and you will fish for people." The men left their nets and followed Jesus. They walked a little while. Then on the shore, they saw two brothers, James and John, in a fishing boat mending their nets. Jesus said to them, "Follow Me."

225
Jesus' First Miracle
JOHN 2:1–11

Jesus and His followers were at a wedding celebration in a town called Cana. Everyone was having fun and eating a big meal. But before the meal was over, they ran out of wine. Mary, Jesus' mother, knew Jesus could help. She said to Him, "There is no wine." Mary told the people, "Do what He tells you."

Nearby were six big stone jars. Each could hold as much water as a bathtub. Jesus said, "Fill those jars with water." Servants did what Jesus said. Then Jesus told them, "Take some of it to the leader of this wedding."

The water had become wine! It was a miracle. This was the first time Jesus did something to prove He was the Son of God. When His followers saw it, they believed in Jesus even more.

226
Jesus Clears the Temple
JOHN 2:13–22

Jesus was in Jerusalem for the Passover. At the temple, He found people selling animals for offerings. Sellers stood at tables, counting their coins. This made Jesus very angry. He chased the people and the animals out of the temple and dumped out the coins. "Take these things out of here!" Jesus shouted. "Stop making My Father's house a marketplace!"

"What right do You have to do this?" the people asked. "Show us a sign that God's given You control of the temple."

"Here's your sign," Jesus said. "Destroy this temple, and in three days I'll raise it up."

"It's taken years to build the temple. It's not finished yet," they answered. "Will You raise it up in three days?"

But Jesus wasn't talking about that temple. He was speaking about His body. One day, they would kill Jesus. Three days later, He would come back to life!

227

"Whoever Believes. . .Will Live Forever"

JOHN 3:1–21

Nicodemus, a leader of a group called the Pharisees—teachers of the law—went to see Jesus.

"We know You're a teacher from God," he said. "No one can do these things unless God is with him."

"I'll tell you the truth," Jesus answered. "No one can see God's kingdom without being born again of the Spirit."

"How can a person be born again?" Nicodemus asked.

"You teach the law," Jesus said, "yet you don't understand. Do you remember that Moses lifted a brass serpent on a pole? Whoever saw it was healed of the snakes' poison."

"Yes," said Nicodemus.

"Well, someday I'll be lifted on a cross. Whoever believes in Me will be healed of sin and have eternal life—be born again. This is because God loves the world so much that He will give His only Son, and whoever believes in Him will live forever."

228
The Woman at the Well
Part One
JOHN 4:7–18

One day, Jesus rested by a well while His followers went to buy food. A woman came to the well to get water. "Give Me a drink," Jesus said.

"You're a Jew," the woman answered. "I'm a Samaritan. Jews don't share with Samaritans."

"You don't know who's asking you for a drink," Jesus told her. "If you did, you'd ask Me, and I'd give you living water. Whoever drinks from this well will get thirsty again. But when I give you living water, the well is inside you. It fills up to give you eternal life."

"Sir," the woman said, "please give me this living water. Then I'll never be thirsty again."

"Go get your husband and come back," Jesus told her.

"I don't have a husband."

"What you say is true," Jesus replied.

229
The Woman at the Well Part Two
JOHN 4:19–42

The woman said, "If You are a prophet, tell me which is right: to worship at this mountain or at Jerusalem?"

Jesus answered, "The time has come when you won't worship the Father in either place. The real worshippers give thanks to Him in spirit and in truth. God wants people who will worship Him this way. God is Spirit. The people who worship Him must believe He is everywhere, although they cannot see Him."

"I believe Christ is coming," said the woman. "He will teach us everything."

Jesus said, "I'm speaking to you. I'm Christ."

She left her water jug at the well and hurried back to her town. "Come and see a man who told me everything I've ever done! Could He be Christ?"

Many people in that town believed in Jesus because of the woman. Jesus stayed there two days. Many more believed because they heard His words.

230

“Your Son Will Live”

JOHN 4:46–54

In a place called Capernaum, there lived a nobleman whose son was very sick. The man heard that Jesus had come from Judea. So he went and found Jesus. “Come and heal my son,” he begged. “He is about to die.”

“Unless you see miracles, you won't believe,” Jesus replied.

The nobleman answered, “Please, sir. Hurry, before he is dead!”

“Go,” Jesus told him. “Your son will live.”

The man believed Jesus' words and started for home. His servants met him on the way. “Your child is alive!” they shouted.

The man asked them what time the boy began to get well. It was at the exact time Jesus had said, “Your son will live.”

The nobleman believed Jesus was the Christ, and so did everyone in his household.

This was the second time Jesus did something to prove He was the Son of God.

231
Trouble in Nazareth Part One
LUKE 4:16–24

At the synagogue—the place of worship—in Jesus' hometown of Nazareth, He read from the book of Isaiah: "The Spirit of the Lord is upon Me. I'm anointed to bring good news to the poor. He has sent Me to call out 'freedom!' to the captives and give sight to the blind; to let the mistreated people go free; and to proclaim the year of God's grace to everyone." When Jesus finished reading, He said, "Today, these words have come true."

Those who heard Him were amazed. But then someone asked, "Isn't this Joseph's son? We know His brothers and sisters. How can He teach us?"

Jesus said, "You are wondering: 'Why doesn't He do miracles like He did in Capernaum?' I'll tell you why. Because a prophet is never welcome in his hometown."

232
Trouble in Nazareth Part Two
LUKE 4:24–32

"It's true," Jesus continued. "A prophet is never welcome in his hometown. In Elijah's time, it didn't rain for three and a half years. There were many who needed help in Israel. But who did God tell Elijah to help? Someone outside Israel. And weren't there many lepers in Israel in Elisha's time? But the only leper the prophet healed was Naaman from Syria."

Jesus' words angered the people in Nazareth. They wanted miracles! They led Jesus up into the hills and planned to throw Him off a cliff. But Jesus got away. It wasn't time yet for Him to die. He went back to Capernaum and taught the people there. They were amazed at His teaching. Unlike other teachers, Jesus spoke like an expert.

233
"You Are the Son of God!"
LUKE 4:33–41

In Capernaum, Jesus met a man controlled by a demon. "Leave us alone, Jesus of Nazareth!" it said. "Have You come to destroy us, Holy One of God?"

Jesus commanded the demon, "Be silent! Come out of him!" The evil spirit threw the man on the ground and left his body. The man wasn't hurt.

Everyone around was amazed. "What kind of speaking is this?" they wondered. "He has power to command the evil spirits. And out they come!"

Later, at Peter's house, Jesus healed Peter's mother-in-law from a high fever. Right away, she got out of bed and served them their meal.

The reports about Jesus were heard everywhere. Sick people came to Jesus. He put His hands on them and cured them. Demons came out of people, shouting, "You are the Son of God!" Jesus wouldn't let the demons speak, because they knew He was Christ.

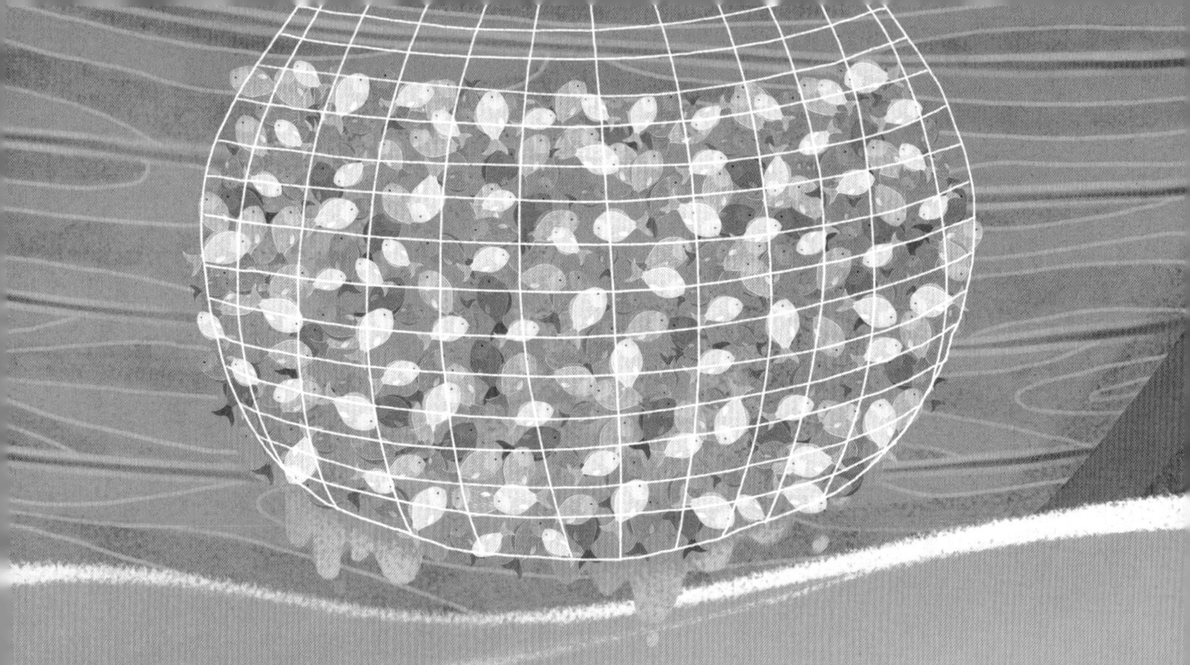

234
"Let Down Your Nets"
LUKE 5:1–11

At the edge of the Sea of Galilee, Peter, Andrew, James, and John had brought in their fishing boats and were busy washing their nets. Jesus stepped into Peter's boat and sat there teaching a crowd of His followers on the beach.

When He finished teaching, Jesus told Peter, "Take the boats to deep water and let down your nets."

"Master," Peter answered, "we've worked all night and caught nothing. But if You say so, I'll let down the nets." When they did, they caught so many fish the nets were breaking. The men filled up their boats with fish!

Amazed, knowing he was with the Christ, Peter fell down and cried, "Go away from me, Lord. I'm a sinful man!"

"Don't be afraid," Jesus told him. "From now on, you'll catch people."

The young men left their boats and everything else behind, and wherever Jesus went, they followed.

235
"Be Made Clean"
LUKE 5:12–16

A man with the skin disease leprosy came to Jesus. He bowed before Him and begged, "If You choose to do so, You can heal me and make my skin clean."

"I do choose this," Jesus said. "Be made clean." Instantly, the leprosy was gone. Jesus ordered the man to tell no one. "Show the priest and make an offering to God," Jesus said.

Before long, the news about Jesus spread. People were amazed when they heard Him speak. Crowds gathered to listen, and people were healed of their diseases.

Sometimes, Jesus needed to go off by Himself for a little while to quiet places where He could pray to His Father, God.

236

"I Have the Power to Forgive Sins"

LUKE 5:17–26

Jesus was inside a house speaking to a crowd. Outside, men came carrying a man on a mat. He couldn't walk. The house was too crowded to bring him through the door. So they went on the roof and made a way to let the paralyzed man down into the house.

When Jesus saw the man, He said, "Friend, your sins are forgiven."

Some Pharisees nearby heard this. They whispered to one another. "No one can forgive sins but God."

Jesus knew their thoughts. "Why do you question this? Is it easier to say: 'Your sins are forgiven,' or 'Stand up and walk?' I want you to know I have the power to forgive sins." Then Jesus spoke to the man: "Stand up, take your mat, and go home." And the man did this, praising God.

Everyone was amazed and praised God. "We've seen great things today," they said.

237
Jesus Works on the Sabbath Part One
JOHN 5:1–18

The Sabbath day was a holy day—a day to rest and honor God. On the Sabbath, Jesus stopped at a pool of water called Bethesda. The water was said to have healing power, and many people went there to be cured.

Jesus spoke to a man who had been sick for thirty-eight years. "Would you like to be made well?" Jesus asked.

"Someone always gets into the pool ahead of me," the man answered.

Jesus said, "Stand up, take your mat, and walk." Instantly, the man was healed! He picked up his mat and walked away.

When the Pharisees heard, they complained to Jesus, "It's against the law to work on the Sabbath."

"My Father works every day, and so do I," Jesus replied.

This made the Pharisees very angry. Jesus spoke as if He were the same as God. The men were so that angry they wanted to hurt Jesus.

238
Jesus Works on the Sabbath Part Two
MARK 3:1–6

Jesus went into the synagogue on the Sabbath. A man was there who had a disabled hand. The people wondered if Jesus would heal again on the Sabbath day. Jesus asked them, "Is it against the law to do good on the Sabbath? What about to do harm? Does your law allow Me to save a life on the Sabbath? How about to kill?"

They didn't answer.

"Stretch out your hand," Jesus said to the man. His hand was perfectly healed!

Seeing this, the Pharisees began making plans with the Romans to destroy Jesus.

239

Jesus Teaches on the Mountain

MATTHEW 5:1–9

Jesus spoke to a huge crowd gathered on a mountainside. His followers—twelve men known as His disciples—were with Him. Jesus taught and spoke blessings to the people:

The poor in spirit are blessed because theirs is the kingdom of heaven.
The meek are blessed because they will inherit the earth.
People who are hungry to do right are blessed because they will be filled.
People who have mercy are blessed because they will be given mercy.
The pure in heart are blessed because they will see God.
Peacemakers are blessed because they will be called children of God.

240
The Centurion's Faith
LUKE 7:1–10

In Capernaum there was a centurion—a leader in the Roman army—whose servant was sick and dying. The centurion wasn't a Jew, like the Israelites, but he was their friend and had helped pay for their synagogue building.

The centurion sent his friends to find Jesus and give Him a message: "Lord, don't trouble Yourself. I don't deserve to have You in my house. If You simply speak the words, my servant will be healed. I'm like You, Lord; someone else tells me what to do. Then I give orders to my soldiers and servants."

Jesus was amazed that the centurion said this. He said to His followers, "I haven't found this kind of faith in all of Israel."

When the centurion's friends returned to him, the servant had already been healed!

241

"I Say to You, Get Up!"

LUKE 7:11–16

Jesus and His disciples traveled to a town called Nain. A huge crowd followed, wanting to see Jesus and hear the words He said. When they arrived at the town gate, they saw a woman crying. Her son had died.

Jesus felt sorry for her. "Don't cry," He said. Then Jesus spoke to the dead man's body: "Young man, I say to you, get up!" Suddenly, the man sat up and began to speak. Jesus gave him to his mother.

The people watching were amazed and frightened when they saw Jesus make a dead man come back to life. "A great prophet has come to us," they said.

242
The Sinful Woman Part One
LUKE 7:36–39

Simon, a Pharisee, invited Jesus to supper. At Simon's house, a woman came with a beautiful little jar of perfume. She kneeled before Jesus and cried. Her tears fell on Jesus' feet. Then the woman dried them with her hair. She kissed His feet and poured perfume on them.

This was a sinful woman. She had done things that God did not like. Everyone in town knew it.

I don't think Jesus is a prophet, Simon said to himself. *If He were, He would know who is touching Him. She's a sinner.*

243
The Sinful Woman Part Two
LUKE 7:40–50

Jesus told a story:

"Two people owed a man money. The first owed five hundred dollars. The other fifty dollars. Neither could pay. The man they owed said they didn't need to pay him back. Which one loved him more?"

Simon answered, "The one who owed the most money."

Jesus said, "You're right. I came to your house. Did you give Me water to wash My feet? No. But the woman bathed My feet in tears and wiped them with her hair. You didn't greet Me with a kiss. But she kissed My feet. You didn't anoint My head with oil. But she anointed My feet with perfume. I tell you, her many sins are forgiven. But the one who's done little to forgive loves little."

Jesus spoke to the woman, "Your sins are forgiven. Your faith has saved you."

Those around Simon's table said, "Who is this who forgives sins?"

244
The Seeds of God's Word
LUKE 8:4–15

Jesus shared this story with His followers:

"A farmer planted seeds. Some seeds fell on a path, and birds ate them. Some fell among rocks. They died without water. Seeds that fell among weeds couldn't grow. But others fell on good soil. Those seeds grew and gave the farmer a good crop."

Later, Jesus explained to His disciples: "The seeds are God's Word. Those on the path are like people who hear God's Word; then the devil takes it from their hearts. They can't believe and be saved. Seeds among rocks are people who believe for a while. But in hard times, they forget God's Word. Seeds fallen among weeds are like people who hear God's Word and ignore it. His Word can't grow, because their hearts are filled with other things. But seeds in good soil—those are God's Word planted in good hearts. Those people's lives are changed forever."

245

The Wind and the Sea Obey Him

MARK 4:35–5:5

At nightfall, Jesus and His disciples were in a boat crossing the Sea of Galilee. Jesus was asleep when a big storm rocked the boat wildly from side to side. His disciples woke Jesus up. "Teacher, don't You care that we're all about to drown?" they cried.

Jesus said to the wind and the sea, "Peace! Be still." Then the wind stopped, and the water became calm. "Why were you afraid?" He asked His disciples. "Do you still have no faith?"

"Who is He?" they asked one another. "Even the wind and the sea obey Him."

246
The Man with an Evil Spirit
MARK 5:6–20

A man with an evil spirit saw Jesus coming. He screamed at Him, "What do You want with me, Jesus, Son of the Most High God?"

"Come out of this man!" Jesus commanded.

"Please, don't make me suffer," the evil spirit said.

"What's your name?" Jesus asked it.

"Our name is Legion because there are many of us inside of him." A herd of pigs grazed nearby. "Let us enter into those pigs," the spirits begged Jesus.

Immediately, the spirits went out of the man. They entered the pigs, and they all ran to the sea and drowned.

When people saw this wild man freed from his evil spirit, they were frightened by Jesus' amazing power. "Go away," they told Him.

Before He left, Jesus said to the man, "Tell your friends what the Lord has done for you." So the man went and told others the good news.

247
“Who Touched Me?”
MARK 5:22–34

A huge crowd followed Jesus. A Jewish leader named Jairus came forward and fell at Jesus' feet. He said, “My little daughter is about to die. Come. Touch her so she will live.” On the way to Jairus's house, the crowd surrounded Jesus on every side.

A woman among the people had had a bleeding problem for twelve years. She said to herself, *If I touch Jesus' robe, He will heal me.* She pushed through the crowd and touched Him. Instantly, her bleeding stopped!

Just then, Jesus felt power go out from Him. “Who touched Me?” He asked.

“How could You know in this crowd?” His disciples answered.

The woman came to Jesus and told Him the story of how even the best doctors and the best medicines couldn't cure her.

“Woman,” He said, “your faith has made you well. Go in peace.”

248
"She's Not Dead; She's Sleeping"
MARK 5:35–43

"Your daughter is dead, Jairus," his friends told him. "Don't bother the Teacher anymore."

Jesus overheard them. "Don't be afraid, Jairus," He said. "Just believe."

Jesus only allowed His disciples Peter, James, and John to go with Him inside Jairus's house. All around Him, people cried. "Why are you crying?" Jesus asked. "She's not dead; she's sleeping."

He went with the girl's parents to the little girl's bedside. Jesus took her hand. "Little girl," He said, "get up." The girl got out of bed, and she started walking around. Those who saw were amazed. "Don't tell anyone what happened," Jesus ordered. "Just give her some food."

249
John the Baptist Dies
MATTHEW 14:1–12; 11:7–15

King Herod was a wicked man. When John the Baptist discovered that Herod had married against the law, he scolded the king. It made Herod so angry that he had John locked up in prison.

On Herod's birthday, there was a big party. His daughter danced for him, and Herod was so pleased, he said, "I'll give you anything you want."

"Ask for John the Baptist to be killed," the girl's mother whispered to her. Herod wasn't sure he wanted to kill John, because John was known as a great prophet. But he gave his daughter what she asked for.

When Jesus heard, He told His disciples, "John was the man the prophet Malachi wrote about when he said, 'Look, I'm sending my messenger ahead of you. He will prepare a way for you.' John did this for Me. No one ever born was greater than John the Baptist."

250
Jesus Feeds the Crowd
MATTHEW 14:13–21

After Jesus heard that John was dead, He went to a quiet place to be alone for a while. When He returned to the shore at the Sea of Galilee, Jesus saw a big crowd waiting for Him. They had been waiting a long time.

"It's late," said the disciples. "Let's send them home so they can eat."

"They don't have to leave," said Jesus. "Give them food."

"All we have is five loaves of bread and two fish," the disciples answered.

Jesus looked up to heaven. Then He blessed the loaves and fish. All at once, there was enough for everyone to eat as much as they wanted! After they ate, the disciples filled twelve more baskets with leftovers.

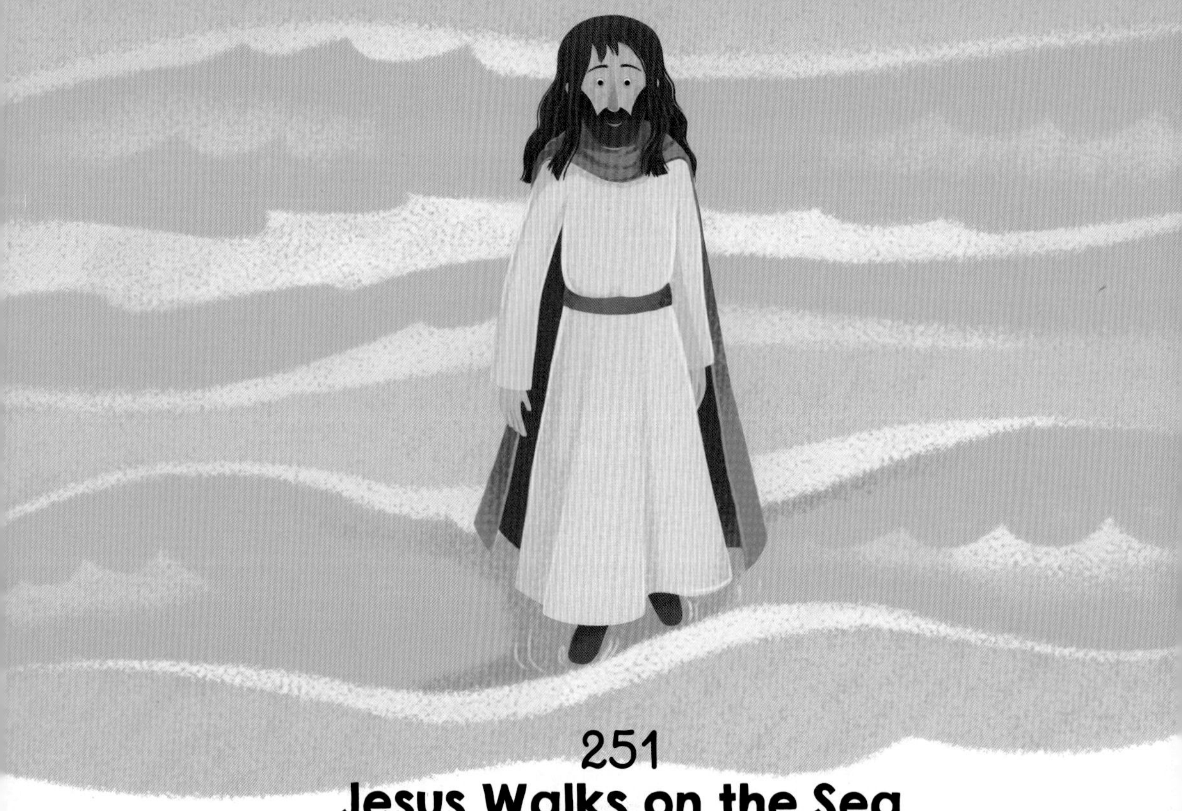

251

Jesus Walks on the Sea

MATTHEW 14:22–33

That night, after the crowd left, Jesus sent His disciples to their boat. Then Jesus went to be alone to pray. When He returned, the boat was far from shore.

The disciples struggled to sail against high winds and strong waves. "Look!" They saw someone walking toward them on the sea. "It's a ghost!" they cried.

"It is I," Jesus said. "Don't be afraid."

Peter wanted to walk on water too. So Jesus held out His hand. "Come," He said.

Peter stepped out of the boat and into the water. He walked toward Jesus. But then he felt afraid and started to sink. "Lord, save me!" he begged.

Safely back in the boat, Jesus stopped the wind and waves. He said to Peter, "You have so little faith. Why did you doubt?"

Then the disciples believed Jesus was truly God's Son, and they worshipped Him.

252
Jesus, the Bread of Life
JOHN 6:25–68

Jesus was teaching a crowd. "I fed you yesterday," He said. "But if you hunger for food that gives you eternal life—forever life—I can give that to you too."

"What do we have to do to get it?" someone asked.

"Believe that God sent Me to save you," Jesus replied.

"We'll believe when we see a miracle!" someone shouted. "God made bread rain from heaven. What can You do?"

Jesus said, "I am the Bread of Life. Whoever comes to Me will never be hungry. Whoever believes in Me will never be thirsty. Your ancestors ate bread from heaven, and still they died. I'm the Living Bread that came down from heaven. Whoever eats this bread will live forever."

Some of His followers didn't understand and left. "Will you leave too?" Jesus asked the disciples.

"Where will we go?" Peter answered. "You speak the words of eternal life."

253
"Even Dogs Get Crumbs"
MATTHEW 15:21–31

When Jesus traveled through a place where Gentiles lived, a woman came to Him and said, "Have mercy on me, Lord! My daughter has an evil spirit inside her."

"This woman is a Gentile, not a Jew!" the disciples reminded Him. "Send her away."

Jesus told the woman, "It wouldn't be right to give to a Gentile what is meant for Jews."

"That's true, Lord," she answered. "But don't even dogs get crumbs that fall from their master's table?"

"Woman, you have great faith!" Jesus said. And He healed her daughter.

Wherever Jesus went, crowds brought sick people to Him, and He cured them. When they saw God heal people and give them the ability to speak, walk, and see, people were amazed, and they praised the God of Israel.

254
"Who Do People Say I Am?"
MATTHEW 16:13–23

Jesus asked His disciples, "Who do people say I am?"

"Some say you're John the Baptist. Others say Elijah, Jeremiah, or another of the prophets."

Jesus said to them, "Who do *you* say I am?"

"You're the Christ, the Son of the living God," Peter answered.

"No man told you this," Jesus replied. "My Father in heaven has shown you. This is the rock on which I'll build My church. You, Peter, are a stone in that building."

Then Jesus told the disciples, "Don't tell anyone I'm the Christ. Soon, I will go to Jerusalem. There I'll suffer and be killed. Three days later, I'll return from death."

"No!" Peter cried. "This mustn't happen to You!"

"If you think that way, Peter, you'll block My plans," Jesus told him. "You see Me as a human king. Understand this: God sent Me so these things could happen."

255
The Voice on the Mountaintop
MATTHEW 17:1–8

Jesus took Peter, James, and John to a mountaintop. There Jesus was changed. His face shone like the sun. His clothing became very bright. Suddenly, Moses and Elijah appeared and spoke with Jesus!

Peter said, "Shall we pitch three tents, Lord? One to worship You, one to worship Moses, and one for Elijah?"

As Peter was talking, a bright cloud covered them. A voice spoke from the cloud: "This is My beloved Son. He pleases Me. Listen to Him!"

The disciples fell to the ground, afraid. When they looked up, only Jesus was there.

256
Faith Makes Everything Possible
MATTHEW 17:14–21

Jesus and His disciples came down the mountain to the crowd.

A man kneeled in front of Jesus. "Lord, have mercy on my son," he said. "An evil spirit controls him. He suffers terribly and falls a lot. I brought him to Your disciples, but they couldn't heal him."

Jesus said to His disciples, "You have no faith. How much longer do I have to put up with you? Bring the boy to Me." Jesus told the spirit to come out, and the boy was healed instantly.

The disciples took Jesus aside and asked, "Why couldn't we do that?"

"Because you have so little faith. You could do so much with just a tiny bit of faith. Faith the size of a mustard seed can move a mountain into the sea. With faith, nothing would be impossible for you."

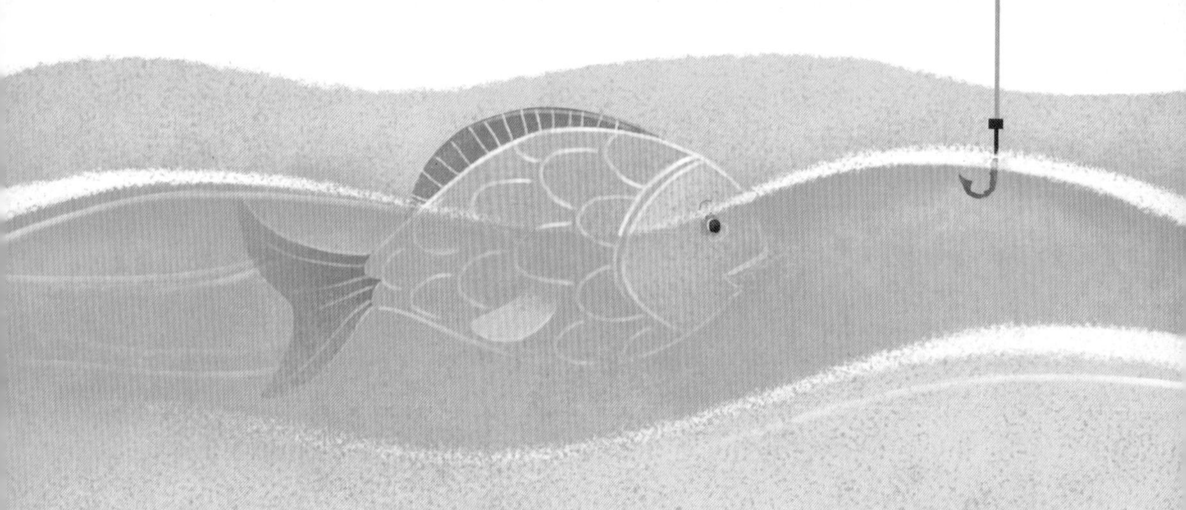

257
The Greatest in the Kingdom
MATTHEW 17:24–18:5

It was tax collection time in the kingdom. Jesus said to His disciples, "From whom do kings collect taxes? Do they take the money from their own children or from others?"

"From others," Peter answered.

"Then the king's children don't pay taxes. However, we don't want to trouble the tax collectors. Go to the sea and fish. When you open the mouth of the first fish you catch, you'll find a coin. It will pay your tax and Mine."

Then the disciples asked Jesus, "Which of us will be greatest in the kingdom of heaven?"

Jesus pointed to a little child. "I'll tell you the truth. Do you want to enter the kingdom? Then you'll have to change and become like a little child. Anyone who is humble like this child is greatest in the kingdom. Anyone who welcomes a child like this welcomes Me."

258
"Forgive Others from Your Heart"
MATTHEW 18:21–35

Peter asked Jesus, "How often should I forgive someone? Seven times?"

Jesus answered, "Not seven times; I tell you: seventy-seven times!" Then Jesus told a story:

"A king's servant owed him a lot of money. The servant couldn't pay. So the king ordered, 'Sell him as a slave to pay for his debt.'

"But the servant begged, 'Please be patient, and I'll pay you everything.' Then the kind king forgave the servant's debt.

"Later, a man owed the servant money. When the man couldn't pay, the servant sent him to jail. The king found out and said, 'You wicked servant! I forgave you your debt because you begged me. I had mercy on you. Shouldn't you have mercy on the one who owes you?'

"Peter," Jesus said, "the lesson is this: My Father is like the king. You are like the servant. You should always forgive others from your heart."

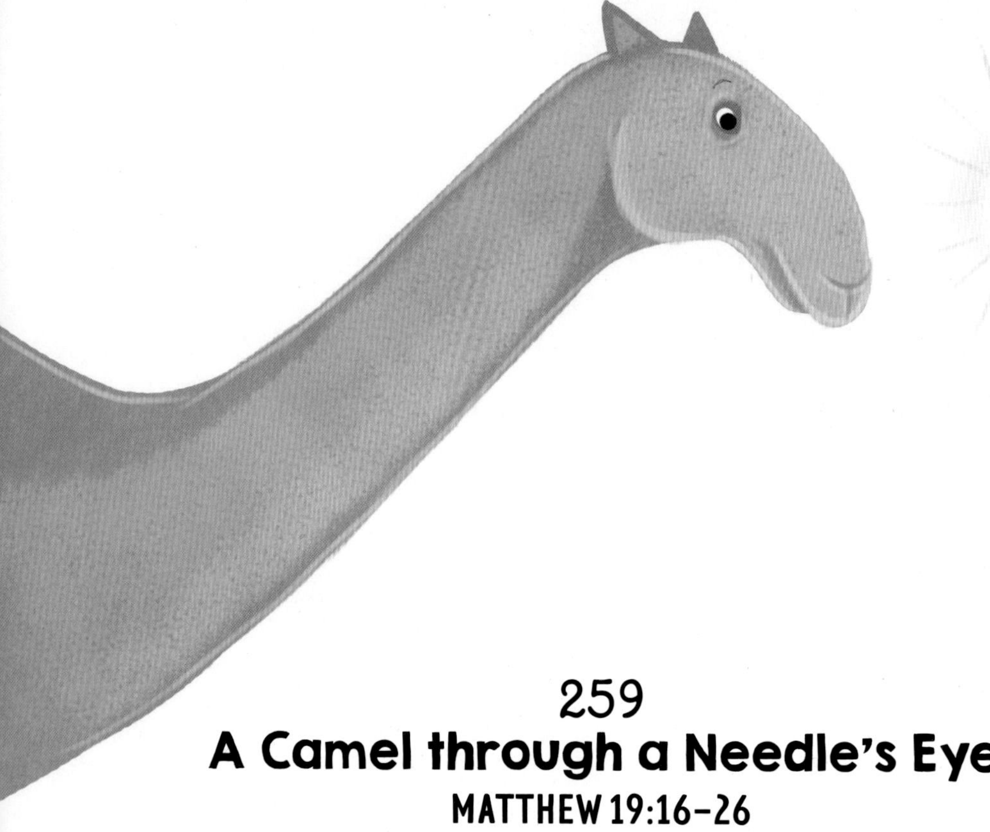

259
A Camel through a Needle's Eye
MATTHEW 19:16–26

A young man asked Jesus, "What do I have to do to have forever life in heaven?"

"Keep the commandments," Jesus answered.

"I've kept all ten. What else is there?"

"Sell everything. Give the money to the poor. Come and follow Me," Jesus told him.

When the young man heard this, he walked away sadly. He was very rich and didn't want to give up everything he had.

Jesus spoke to His disciples: "Can a camel go through a needle's eye? That's how hard it is for the rich to enter the kingdom."

"So, who can be saved?" they wondered.

"It's impossible for people to save themselves," Jesus answered. "But God can do anything."

260

The One Thing That's Needed

LUKE 10:38–42

One day, Jesus was visiting His friends Mary and Martha at their house. Mary sat near Jesus, listening to Him talk. But Martha was busy preparing a meal and being a good host for their guest.

Martha said to Jesus, "My sister has left all the work for me to do. Does that bother You at all?"

Jesus answered, "Martha, Martha, you are worried about so many things. But there's only one thing that's really needed. Mary has chosen to love Me, and I won't stop her."

261
The Blind Man Sees Part One
JOHN 9:1–9

Jesus and His disciples saw a blind man begging in the streets. "Teacher," the disciples asked, "whose fault is it that he is blind? Did his parents sin, or did his sin cause this?"

"He was born blind for a reason," Jesus answered. "This has nothing to do with anyone's sin. God wants to work in him. We must do God's work while it's day. Night is coming when no one can work. As long as I'm in the world, I'm the Light of the world."

Jesus spit on the ground and made mud. He rubbed it on the man's eyes. "Go," He said. "Wash your eyes in the pool in Siloam." The man did as Jesus said. For the first time in his life, he could see!

When he heard neighbors asking, "Isn't this the man who used to sit and beg?" he told them, "Yes, I'm that man."

262

The Blind Man Sees Part Two

JOHN 9:10–25

They took the man, who could now see, to the Pharisees because he had been healed on the Sabbath when no one was supposed to work.

The man who had been blind told them, "Jesus made mud. He spread it on my eyes and said, 'Wash at Siloam Pool.' I think He's a prophet."

The Pharisees didn't believe him. "Maybe he was never blind," they said. So they asked his parents.

"This is our son," they answered. "He was born blind. We don't know why he can see."

The Pharisees said to the man, "You should only praise God that you can see. Jesus made mud on the Sabbath. He's a sinner, not a miracle worker."

"I don't know if He's a sinner," the man answered. "But I do know that once I was blind, and now I can see."

263
The Blind Man Sees Part Three
JOHN 9:26–41

"I've told you, Jesus gave me my sight," said the once blind beggar. "Do you want to be His follower like me?"

"No!" the Pharisees answered. "You follow Jesus, but we follow Moses. We know God spoke to Moses. We don't know where Jesus comes from."

"That's amazing!" exclaimed the man. "You don't know where Jesus comes from? He opened my eyes! Everybody knows God doesn't listen to sinners. God listens to those who worship and obey Him. Since the world began, no one born blind could see. If Jesus wasn't from God, He couldn't do this."

"Who are you to teach us?" said the Pharisees. Then they threw the man out.

When Jesus heard this, He went looking for the man. When He found him, Jesus asked, "Do you believe in the Son of God? He's speaking with you right now."

"Lord, I believe," said the man. And he worshipped Jesus.

264
Jesus, the Good Shepherd
JOHN 10:1–39

Jesus tried to explain why the once blind man followed Him: "A shepherd keeps his sheep safe in a barn. He enters the barn through the door. Strangers who want to steal the sheep sneak in by other ways. The sheep know their shepherd's voice. They won't follow a stranger."

When the people didn't understand, Jesus said: "I'm the barn door. Those who enter through Me will be saved. I come to give forever life. I'm the Good Shepherd who gives His life for the sheep. I know My sheep, and they know Me—just like the Father knows Me, and I know My Father."

"God isn't Your father! You're human." Some of the Jews picked up stones to throw at Jesus.

"I've done many of My Father's good works. Is this why you want to hurt Me?" Jesus asked.

When they tried to arrest Him, Jesus escaped.

265
Jesus and the Lawyer Part One
LUKE 10:1–28

Jesus sent seventy disciples, in pairs, to every town He would soon visit. "I send you like lambs among wolves. There are some who want to hurt Me," He said. "When people welcome you to town, eat food they offer. Cure their sick. Tell them, 'The kingdom of God has come near you.' Whoever listens to you listens to Me. If they turn you away, they've turned Me away."

The disciples returned, filled with joy. "Lord, in Your name even the evil spirits obey us!"

"Don't rejoice over this," Jesus said. "Instead, rejoice that your names are written in heaven."

A man who studied Jewish law asked Jesus, "What should I do to get life that lasts forever?"

"What does the law say?" asked Jesus.

"Love God with your whole heart," answered the lawyer. "And love your neighbor like you love yourself."

"That's right. Do this, and you'll have life," said Jesus.

266
Jesus and the Lawyer Part Two
LUKE 10:29–37

The lawyer knew the Jewish law well. It said to love your neighbor. But he didn't always do that—he was human, after all. So he tried to find a way around the law by asking Jesus, "Who is my neighbor?"

Jesus answered with a story: "A traveling man was robbed and beaten by criminals. As he lay on the road, a priest walked by. So did a Levite. But a Samaritan was the only one who stopped to help. He washed and bandaged the traveler's wounds and carried him to a nearby inn. This Samaritan paid the innkeeper to care for the man. Which of these three was the traveler's neighbor?"

"The man who helped," the lawyer answered.

"Right," said Jesus. "Go and do the same." Jesus said these words to teach the lawyer that doing what God says is more important than the law.

267
Jesus and Lazarus Part One
JOHN 11:1–24

Lazarus, Mary and Martha's brother, was very sick. The women sent a message to Jesus, believing He would come right away and heal the man. But Jesus waited two days. Then He told His disciples, "Our friend Lazarus has fallen asleep. I'm going to Judea to awaken him."

The disciples didn't understand. They said, "Well, Lord, if he's only asleep, he'll be fine." They didn't want to go to Judea where Lazarus lived. Some of the people there wanted to kill Jesus.

Jesus and His disciples went anyway. When they arrived, Lazarus had already been dead four days. Martha ran to meet Jesus. "If You'd been here," she said, "Lazarus wouldn't have died. But I know God will give You anything You ask."

"Your brother will return from death," Jesus answered.

"I know, Lord," said Martha. "He will rise with all the dead on resurrection day, at the end of time."

268
Jesus and Lazarus Part Two
JOHN 11:25–37

"Martha, I am the Resurrection and the Life," said Jesus. "Those who believe in Me may die, but they'll live again. Do you believe this?"

Martha didn't understand. She replied, "Yes. I believe You're Christ, God's Son, who has come into the world." Then she hurried home to her sister.

"Mary," said Martha, "Jesus is here. He wants to see you."

Mary went to Jesus and kneeled at His feet, crying. "Lord, You should have been here. Then Lazarus wouldn't have died." It troubled Jesus to see Mary crying. He cried too. Some people who stood nearby watching said, "See how much He loved Lazarus?" But others said, "He made the blind man see. Couldn't He have kept this man from dying?"

"Where did you bury Lazarus?" Jesus asked Mary.

"Come and see, Lord," she said.

269
Jesus and Lazarus Part Three
JOHN 11:38–53

A crowd followed Jesus and the sisters to Lazarus's tomb. A huge rock blocked the entrance. "Remove it," Jesus said to some men nearby. They rolled away the stone.

"Lord," Martha warned, "his body has been dead for days. Surely it will smell bad."

"Martha," Jesus said, "I told you to believe and you will see God's glory." Then Jesus prayed, "Thank You, Father. You've heard Me." Jesus said this so the people who heard would believe in Him. Then, in a loud voice, Jesus said: "Lazarus, come out!"

Lazarus walked out of the tomb. The crowd gasped, "He's alive!" Many believed then that Jesus was the Christ, God's Son. When the Pharisees heard this, they were worried. "Soon everyone will believe in Jesus," they said. So they planned to kill Him.

270
Set Free on the Sabbath
LUKE 13:10–17

On the Sabbath, Jesus was teaching in the synagogue. A woman came in. She was bent over and could not stand up straight. Jesus called to her, "Woman, you are set free from your disability." He touched her, and she stood straight and tall as she gave thanks to God.

The synagogue's religious leader was furious that Jesus healed someone on the Sabbath. It was against the law to work on the Sabbath day. The leader spoke to the crowd: "Come during the week to be cured, not on the holy day."

Jesus replied, "You faker! You untie your donkeys on the Sabbath and set them free to drink. Satan has disabled this woman for eighteen years. Shouldn't she be set free on the Sabbath?"

When Jesus said this, He put the religious leader to shame. The entire crowd was happy that they saw the wonderful thing Jesus did.

271
Jesus Welcomes Sinners Part One
LUKE 15:1–7

Everyone was interested in hearing what Jesus had to say. Huge crowds gathered to see Him. And Jesus welcomed them all, even the tax collectors and those considered to be bad people.

"Look at Him," Pharisees and other religious people complained. "He welcomes sinners and even eats with them!"

When Jesus heard this, He told them a story: "Suppose you have a hundred sheep and lost one. Don't you leave the other ninety-nine to search for the lost sheep? When you find it, you bring it home, and you are happy. You say to your friends, 'Be glad with me! I've found my lost sheep.' So listen to Me. There's great joy in heaven when one sinner turns away from sin. Much more than over ninety-nine people who keep the law like you."

272
Jesus Welcomes Sinners Part Two
LUKE 15:11–24

Jesus told another story to explain that God celebrates when a sinner comes to Him:

"A man gave equal parts of his property to his two sons. The younger son took his share and went to a faraway land. He spent his money foolishly until, one day, he couldn't afford food. *My father's servants have food*, he thought. *But here I am starving! I'm going home. I'll say, 'Father, I've sinned against heaven and against you. If you don't want me as your son anymore, I will work for food.'* He set off for home.

"When his father saw him, he ran to his son and hugged him. 'Father,' the son said, 'I've sinned against you—'

"But his father interrupted, calling to his servants: 'Bring my best clothes for him. Let's eat and celebrate! My son was dead, and now he's alive. He was lost, and now he's found.' "

273
Jesus Welcomes Sinners Part Three
LUKE 15:25–32

Jesus continued His story:

"The older son had been wise with his spending. When he heard his younger brother had come home to a big celebration, he was angry. He felt even worse when his father asked him to join in the feast.

" 'Father!' he said. 'While my brother was away, I worked for you. I've worked like a slave and never disobeyed you. But you've given me not even a little party with my friends. Now my brother comes back. He's wasted your property in sin. And you throw a huge feast!'

"His father answered, 'Son, you are always with me. Everything that's mine is yours. We must celebrate and rejoice for your brother. He was dead, and now he has come to life. He was lost and has been found.' "

Jesus told these stories because He wanted the law keepers to understand why God (and Jesus) loves sinners.

274
Lazarus and the Rich Man
LUKE 16:19–31

Jesus said:

"There was a rich man with fine clothes and good food to eat. Another man, Lazarus, begged for food in the street. His body was covered with sores.

"When Lazarus died, angels carried him to Abraham in heaven. When the rich man died, he felt nothing but heat and misery. From far away, he saw Abraham with Lazarus. 'Abraham, have mercy,' he cried. 'Send Lazarus with water. I'm miserable in all this heat.'

"Abraham answered, 'In life you had good things. Lazarus didn't. Now he's comfortable, and you're suffering. No one can come back.'

" 'Then, send Lazarus to warn my brothers so they won't end up like me,' the rich man said. 'If someone comes from the dead, they'll surely listen.'

" 'Abraham had the final word: 'If they haven't listened to the words of Moses and the prophets, they won't listen to a dead man either.' "

275
Parables—Stories That Teach
LUKE 18:1–14

Jesus often told parables—stories that teach. Like this one:

There was a judge who didn't respect people or God. A woman needed a fair judgment in her case, but the judge wasn't fair.

"The law says you must be fair," the woman said. She kept coming back to the judge, expecting him to judge fairly. She became such a bother that he gave her a fair judgment just to be rid of her. If an uncaring judge ends up being fair, think about how much fairer God is to those who keep asking and praying.

Jesus told another parable: "A Pharisee and tax collector both prayed. The Pharisee said, 'Thank You that I'm religious and not like that tax collector.' The tax collector prayed, 'Have mercy on me. I'm a sinner.' Which man did God accept? The tax collector! Praise yourself, and you'll be humbled. Humble yourself, and you'll be honored."

276
"Let the Little Children Come"
LUKE 18:15–17

Parents brought their little children to Jesus. They wanted Him to bless them. When His disciples saw this, they told the parents to stop bothering Jesus.

But Jesus said, "Let the children come to Me. Don't stop them. The kingdom of God belongs to those like these little ones." He held the babies and gently blessed the children. Then Jesus turned to the grown-ups and said, "I'll tell you the truth: You must receive the kingdom like a child. If not, you will never enter into it."

277
"Your Faith Has Saved You"
LUKE 18:35–43

When a blind man named Bartimaeus sat near the Jericho Road begging, he heard someone say, "Jesus is walking by."

"Jesus!" Bartimaeus shouted. "Have mercy on me!" The people in front ordered him to be quiet. But Bartimaeus only shouted louder. "Jesus, have mercy on me!" Jesus stopped walking. He told His disciples to bring the man to Him.

"What do you want Me to do for you?" Jesus asked Bartimaeus.

"Lord, let me see again," he answered.

Then Bartimaeus heard Jesus say, "Receive your sight. Your faith has saved you." Instantly, Bartimaeus could see! He followed Jesus, praising God with all the people.

278

Jesus and Zacchaeus

LUKE 19:1–10

Jesus was coming! A rich man, a tax collector named Zacchaeus, was too short to see over the crowd near the road, so he climbed up into a tree. From there, Zacchaeus had a perfect view of Jesus when He walked by.

Imagine how surprised Zacchaeus was when Jesus stopped, looked up at him, and said, "Zacchaeus, come down. I'm going to stay at your house today."

Zacchaeus hurried down the tree. "Lord," he said, "half of all I own I'll give to the poor. If I've cheated anyone, I'll pay them back four times as much."

Some of the people grumbled, "Jesus is going to stay in the house of a sinner!"

When Jesus heard this, He said, "Today, salvation has come to Zacchaeus's house. He is an ancestor of Abraham, just as you are. Remember, the Son of God came to seek out and save the lost sinners."

279

"What a Waste!"

MATTHEW 26:6–13

Jesus and His disciples were staying in a town called Bethany. While they sat at a table eating, a woman came with a small jar of very expensive perfume. She didn't have much money, and perfume like hers was worth a lot. It was the custom then to honor special guests by gently pouring oil or a spicy perfume on their heads. While the disciples watched, this woman poured her perfume onto Jesus' head to honor Him as Lord.

"What a waste of her money!" the disciples said.

"Don't say that," Jesus told them. "She's done a good thing. I won't always be here. She's prepared My body for burial. Listen: The Gospel—the good news about what I've done—will be preached all over the world. Then what this woman has done for Me will be remembered."

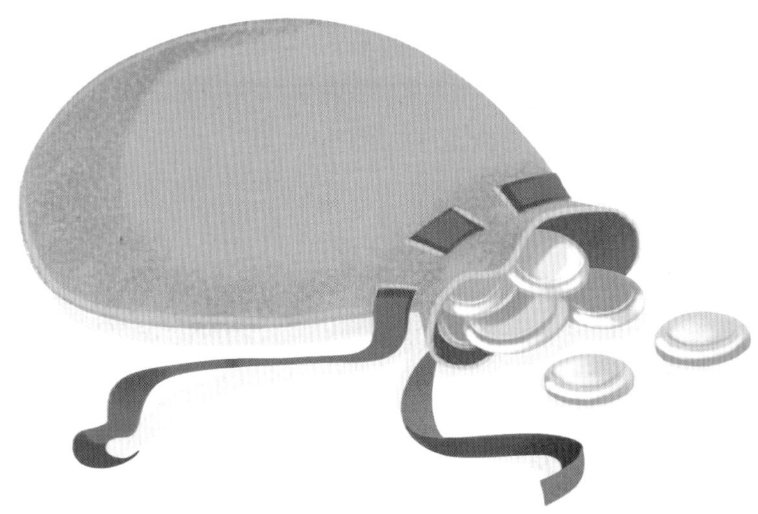

280
"Your King Is Humbly Coming"
MATTHEW 21:1–11; 26:14–16; LUKE 19:29–35

Jesus was traveling from Bethany to Jerusalem. As they neared the city, Jesus told His disciples to bring a donkey for Him to ride on. He told them exactly where to find it. Long before Jesus was born, Zechariah the prophet had said this would happen. He said: "Look, Jerusalem, your King is humbly coming to you. He is riding on a donkey."

One of Jesus' disciples, Judas, went ahead of Jesus to Jerusalem. He asked the priests there, "What will you pay me if I lead you to arrest Jesus?" They paid Judas thirty pieces of silver. From that moment, Judas looked for a chance to turn Jesus over to His enemies.

281
"Hosanna in the Highest Heaven!"
LUKE 19:36–44

As Jesus rode down from the Mount of Olives and into Jerusalem, people covered the path with their coats. Others spread leaves from palm trees. As He came nearer, Jesus' followers praised God and shouted, "Blessed is the King who comes in the name of the Lord! Hosanna in the highest heaven!"

Some of the Pharisees warned Jesus, "Tell Your followers not to say such things!"

But Jesus answered, "Even if the people were silent, the stones would shout."

Then Jesus cried. He wept for Jerusalem, saying, "A time is coming when your enemies will destroy you. They will tear you down. Not one stone will be left on another. This is because you did not notice when God visited you."

282
The House of Prayer
MATTHEW 21:12–17; MARK 11:15–19

In Jerusalem, Jesus saw that people had set up tables inside the temple and were selling things. This made Him angry. He went inside and knocked over their tables and chairs. Then He said in a loud voice: "It is written in the scriptures, 'My house will be called a house of prayer, but you are making it a den of robbers.'" The priests heard what Jesus did. They kept looking for a way to kill Him. But they were afraid of Jesus. The blind and disabled came to Him, and He cured them.

When the priests heard children joyfully shouting in the temple, "Hosanna to the Son of God!" they were upset.

"Do you hear what these children are saying?" they asked Jesus.

Jesus answered, "It says in the scriptures, 'Praise has come from the mouths of little children and babies.' Don't you know that?"

283
The Story of the Vineyard
MATTHEW 21:33–46

Jesus said to the priests:

"A man rented his vineyard, where he grew grapes, to another man and his workers. At harvest, the owner's servants came to collect his share. But the renters beat the servants. The owner sent more servants, but the renters beat them too. Finally, the owner sent his son. But when the renters saw him coming, they said, 'Someday this vineyard will be his. Let's kill him. Then the land will be ours.' "

Jesus said, "Now answer this: When the owner comes, what will he do to those renters?"

"He'll put them to death," the priests replied. "He'll rent the vineyard to people who will give him his fair share."

"Right," said Jesus. "So God's kingdom will be taken away from you. It will be given to people who produce the kingdom's fruit."

The priests knew Jesus was talking about them, and they wanted to arrest Him.

284
The Story of the Wedding Feast
MATTHEW 22:1–14

Jesus told another story:

"A king planned a wedding feast for his son. He sent his servants to bring the guests, but the guests wouldn't come. The king said, 'Tell them everything is ready; come and enjoy the feast.' But the guests embarrassed the king and hurt his servants. So the king sent his soldiers to destroy them and their city.

"Then the king told his servants, 'Go into the streets. Invite everyone to my son's celebration.' The servants invited both good and bad people, and many came.

"At the feast, the king noticed a man not dressed to attend a wedding. 'Sir,' he said, 'how did you get in without wedding clothes?' The man said nothing. 'Tie him up,' commanded the king. 'Throw him out into the darkness where there are people sad and crying.' "

Jesus ended His story by saying, "Many are called, but few are chosen."

285
Giving to God
MATTHEW 22:15–22; MARK 12:41–44

The Pharisees were in charge of the Jewish religion, and the Romans ruled the land. Both wanted to trick Jesus to prove He wasn't the Christ. "Teacher," they said, "we know You teach God's way. Tell us: should we pay taxes to the emperor?"

"Why are you testing Me?" asked Jesus. "Show Me a coin that you'd use to pay taxes." They brought Him a Roman coin. "Whose picture is on this coin?" Jesus asked.

"The emperor's," they answered.

"Right," said Jesus. "So give the emperor what belongs to him. And give God what belongs to God."

Later, Jesus taught His disciples more about giving to God. They stood where people brought money for the temple. Rich people brought much. A poor woman brought two pennies. Jesus said, "This woman has given more than all the others put together. They have plenty to give. She has nothing, but she gave everything she has."

286

The Story of the Ten Bridesmaids

MATTHEW 24:1–3; 25:1–13

Jesus' disciples said, "Teacher, look at these beautiful temple buildings."

"All this will be destroyed," Jesus said.

"When will this happen?" the disciples wondered.

Jesus answered with a story:

"Ten bridesmaids with lamps waited to meet the bridegroom. Five were foolish, five wise. The wise had extra oil for their lamps, but the foolish had none. At midnight, someone shouted, 'Here comes the bridegroom!'

"The foolish bridesmaids' oil had run out. 'Give us oil to light our lamps,' they begged.

" 'Go buy your own,' said the others.

"While the foolish were out buying oil, the bridegroom took the wise to his wedding feast and shut the door. When the foolish arrived, they said, 'Lord, open the door.'

"But the bridegroom answered, 'I don't know who you are.'

"So be alert," Jesus said. "You don't know the day or the hour when your Lord will come."

287
Jesus Tells of Returning to Heaven
MATTHEW 25:31–26:2

Jesus said to His disciples, "When I return to heaven, I'll sit on a glorious throne, and all earth's nations will gather there. I'll divide people into two groups. I'll say to those on the right, 'Come here. You're blessed by My Father. Here's the kingdom He has waiting for you. I was hungry, and you gave Me food. I was thirsty, and you gave Me something to drink. I was a stranger, and you welcomed Me. You gave Me clothes, and you visited Me.'

"Those people will ask, 'When did we do this?'

"I'll say, 'The way you treated others is how you treated Me.'

"To the people on the left, I'll say, 'Get away from Me! You're not welcome in heaven. You did nothing for others, so you did nothing for Me.' "

Then Jesus told them, "The Passover is in two days. Then I'll be arrested and hung on a cross."

288
The Last Supper
LUKE 22:7–20; MATTHEW 26:26–28

The time came to celebrate the Passover. Peter and John prepared the feast in a house in Jerusalem. Then Jesus and His disciples ate together in a large upstairs room.

"I've been looking forward to this Passover," Jesus said. "I want to eat this meal with you before I suffer." Then He took a loaf of bread, broke it into pieces, and gave some to each disciple. "Take and eat this. It represents My body, which is broken for you," He said. Then Jesus passed around a cup of wine. "Each of you, drink some of this," He said. "It represents the blood that I will shed for forgiveness of sins."

289
Jesus Washes the Disciples' Feet
JOHN 13:4–16

When He finished eating, Jesus got up from the table and poured water into a pan. He brought a towel and began washing His disciples' feet. Usually, servants would wash their masters' feet to clean off the dirt from wearing sandals.

Peter said, "Master, why are You going to wash my feet? No!"

Jesus answered, "You don't understand why I'm doing this. But later you'll see. Unless I wash your feet, you don't belong to Me. You call Me 'Lord' and 'Master,' yet I've washed your feet. So you should do the same to one another. The servants are not greater than their master."

290
"One of You Will Betray Me"
JOHN 13:21–38

"One of you will turn Me over to those who hate Me," Jesus said.

The disciples looked at one another, wondering. "Lord," asked John, "who is it?"

"The one to whom I give this piece of bread." Jesus gave the bread to Judas. "Do what you're going to do quickly."

After Judas took the bread, he hurried out into the night.

None of the disciples knew why Jesus said this. Some thought Jesus wanted Judas to buy something for the festival.

"I'll only be with you a little longer," said Jesus. "Here's a new commandment for you. Love one another just as I've loved you. You cannot come to the place I'm going. But you'll follow afterward."

Peter said, "Lord, why can't I follow You now? I'll do anything for You—even die!"

"I'll tell you what you'll really do. Listen for the rooster to crow tomorrow morning. By then, you'll have rejected Me three times."

291
A Garden Called Gethsemane
MATTHEW 26:30–46

After supper that night, Jesus and His disciples sang a hymn together and then went to the Mount of Olives. At a garden called Gethsemane, Jesus said to them, "Sit here while I go to pray." He took Peter, James, and John with Him. "I am very sad," He told them. "Stay awake with Me here."

Then Jesus went by Himself a little bit away from them where He could be alone. He begged God, "My Father, don't make Me do this. But I know this is what You want. So I will do it."

When He returned to His disciples, Jesus found them sleeping. "Get up!" He told them. "Let's go. It's time for Me to be betrayed."

292

Jesus Is Arrested

MATTHEW 26:47–56

Judas was coming. With him was a crowd carrying torches, clubs, and swords. The religious leaders had sent them to arrest Jesus. Judas's job was to lead them to Him.

"He is the one I'll kiss," Judas said. When he saw Jesus, Judas walked up to Him and said, "Hello, Teacher!" Then Judas kissed Jesus' face.

"Friend," said Jesus, "do what you came to do."

Jesus addressed the crowd, "You've come to arrest Me with swords and clubs. Am I a criminal? I've been with you each day teaching in the temple. You didn't arrest Me there."

When the disciples saw Jesus arrested, they ran from the garden. Then the crowd led Jesus away.

293
A Rooster Crows
LUKE 22:54–62

In the darkness, they took Jesus into the high priest's house. Outside, the crowd waited. Peter was among them. Light from torches glowed all around.

A woman recognized Peter's face. "He was with Jesus," she said.

"Woman," said Peter, "I don't know Him."

Later, someone else said, "You're His follower."

"No, I am not," Peter lied.

Then someone insisted, "He's from Galilee. I know this man was with Jesus."

"No!" Peter answered. "I don't know what you're talking about."

It was almost dawn. Peter heard a rooster crow. Jesus had said this would happen—by the time the rooster crowed, Peter would deny Him three times. When Peter remembered this, he walked away and cried.

294

"He Should Die!"

LUKE 22:63–71

Jesus' enemies mocked Him. They blindfolded and beat Him. Then, when morning came, the leaders and head priests gathered, and guards brought Jesus to them.

"If You are the Christ, tell us," they said.

Jesus answered, "If I tell you, you won't believe Me. If I ask you questions, you won't answer. But from now on, I'll be seated at the right hand of God's throne."

"Are You saying that You're the Son of God?" they asked.

"You say that I am," Jesus answered.

"There!" said one of the leaders. "You heard Him say it. And for saying He is the Son of God, He should die."

So they tied Jesus up and led Him away.

295
Judas Dies
MATTHEW 27:3–10

When Judas heard they planned to kill Jesus, he was sorry for what he had done. He went to the priests and tried to give back the thirty pieces of silver they'd given him to betray Jesus. "I've sinned!" Judas told them. "Jesus has done nothing wrong."

"What you've done is your problem—not ours," they said to Judas.

So he threw the silver at them. Then Judas ran away. Judas hated so much what he had done that he took his own life.

The priests didn't know what to do with the silver. It wouldn't be right to give it to the temple as an offering to God. So they used it to buy a potter's field—a cemetery where those who weren't Jewish would be buried. Many years before, the prophet Jeremiah had said this would happen.

296
"This Man Is Innocent"
LUKE 23:1–7; JOHN 18:28–38

A man named Pontius Pilate was the Roman ruler in Jerusalem. The priests and leaders took Jesus to his palace to be judged. They said to Pilate, "This man says that He, not the emperor, is our king."

"Are You the king of the Jews?" Pilate asked Jesus.

"You say I'm a king," Jesus answered. "But I came for one reason: to bring the truth."

"And what is the truth?" Pilate asked. He didn't understand what Jesus meant. Then Pilate told the leaders and priests, "This man has done nothing wrong."

"Still," they insisted, "He upsets people everywhere—from Galilee to Jerusalem."

"Herod is in charge in Galilee," said Pilate. "So take Him to Herod."

297
"Crucify Him! Crucify Him!"
LUKE 23:8–25

The leaders and priests took Jesus to Herod. The king and his soldiers shamed Jesus and mocked Him. Then Herod sent Jesus back to Pilate. Jesus wore a royal robe that Herod's men had put on Him, making fun of the idea that He was a king.

A crowd gathered. "This man hasn't done anything wrong," Pilate told them. "He's done nothing worth dying for."

"Crucify Him!" they shouted. "Let Barabbas the murderer go free instead. Crucify Jesus!"

Pilate tried one more time to save Jesus' life, but the people kept shouting. So Pilate let the murderer, Barabbas, out of prison. Then Pilate allowed his soldiers to whip Jesus, and he turned Jesus over to the angry crowd.

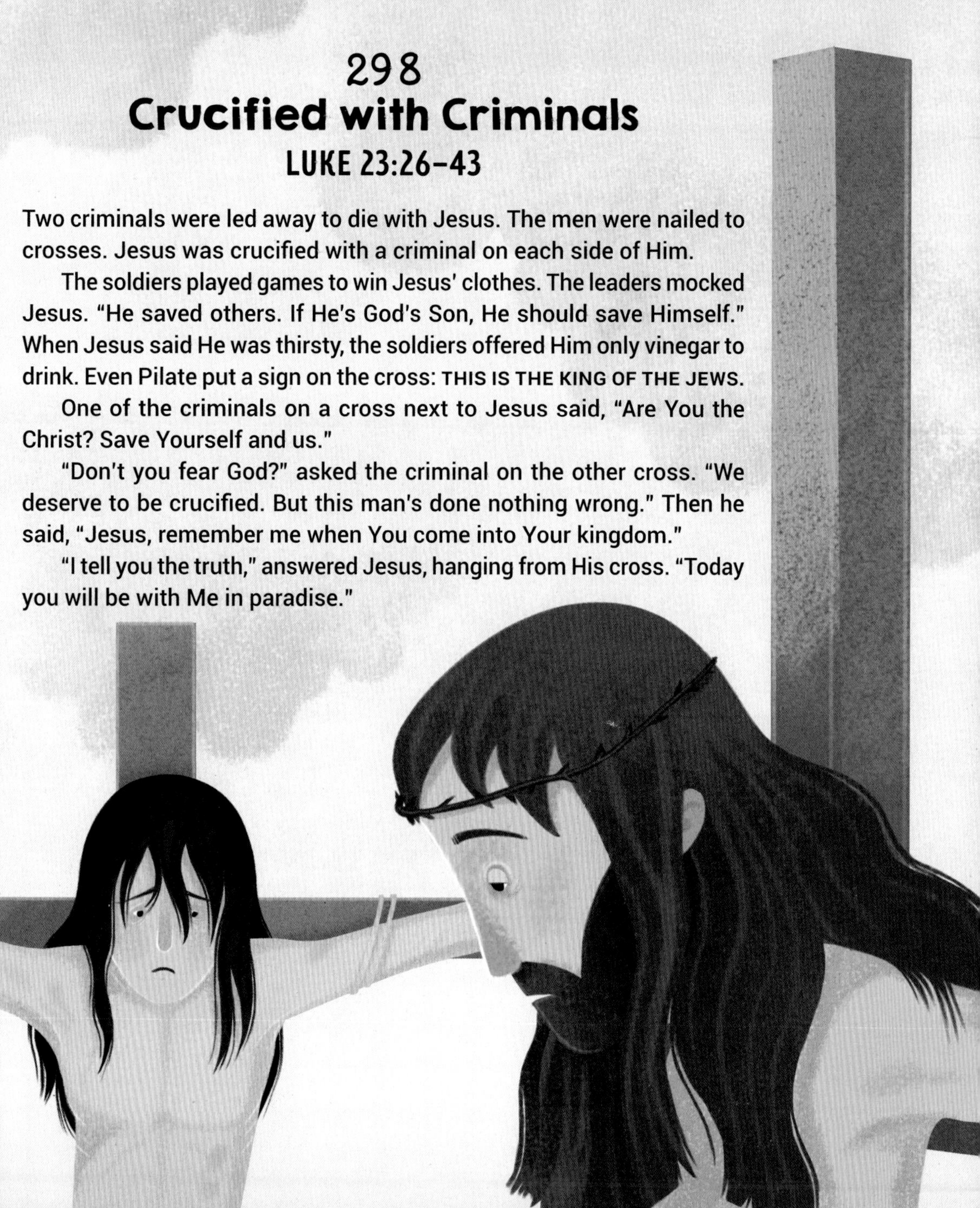

298
Crucified with Criminals
LUKE 23:26–43

Two criminals were led away to die with Jesus. The men were nailed to crosses. Jesus was crucified with a criminal on each side of Him.

The soldiers played games to win Jesus' clothes. The leaders mocked Jesus. "He saved others. If He's God's Son, He should save Himself." When Jesus said He was thirsty, the soldiers offered Him only vinegar to drink. Even Pilate put a sign on the cross: THIS IS THE KING OF THE JEWS.

One of the criminals on a cross next to Jesus said, "Are You the Christ? Save Yourself and us."

"Don't you fear God?" asked the criminal on the other cross. "We deserve to be crucified. But this man's done nothing wrong." Then he said, "Jesus, remember me when You come into Your kingdom."

"I tell you the truth," answered Jesus, hanging from His cross. "Today you will be with Me in paradise."

299
Jesus Dies
MATTHEW 27:45–54; JOHN 19:30

Although it was daytime, the sky became dark as Jesus hung on His cross. Darkness continued from noon to three that afternoon. Then Jesus loudly cried, "My God, My God, why have You left Me?" People thought Jesus was calling to Elijah the prophet. Then Jesus said, "It is finished." He stopped breathing.

At that moment, the curtain in the temple ripped from top to bottom. This opened the special holy place in the temple—the place only the most important priest was allowed to enter. An earthquake rumbled across the land, and rocks split open.

When the captain of the Roman guards saw these things, he was terrified. "Absolutely, this man was God's Son," he said.

300
A Tomb in a Rock
MATTHEW 27:57–66; JOHN 19:38–42

A man named Joseph from Arimathea took Jesus' body from the cross. Together with Nicodemus, he wrapped Jesus' body in spices and clean cloths. They laid it in a new tomb Joseph had cut in the side of a rock. A heavy stone was rolled to block the tomb's door, and then the men left.

The leading priests and Pharisees went to Pilate and said, "That liar, Jesus, said He would come back from death in three days. Send soldiers to guard the tomb so His disciples can't come and steal His body." So Pilate had the tomb sealed, and he sent guards to watch over it.

301

"He Has Risen!"

MATTHEW 28:1–7

It was Sunday morning, the third day after Jesus had died on the cross. The sun shone brightly when Mary from Bethany and Mary Magdalene came to Jesus' tomb. Suddenly, an earthquake shook the earth! An angel rolled away the stone that sealed Jesus' tomb, and the angel sat by the opening, his robes flashing like lightning. The guards fell down because they were so afraid.

The angel spoke to the women. "Don't be frightened. I know you're looking for Jesus. He isn't here. He has risen, just as He said He would. Here, look where He lay." The tomb was empty! "Quickly, go tell His disciples that: Jesus is waiting for them in Galilee. They should meet Him there."

302
"I've Seen the Lord!"
JOHN 20:1–18

Mary Magdalene stood alone, crying by Jesus' tomb. She turned and saw someone standing there. Could it be Jesus? Mary said to herself, *Maybe it's just the gardener.* "Sir," she said, "have you taken away my Lord? Tell me where you've laid Him."

Then she heard a familiar voice. "Mary."

"Jesus!" she cried, moving toward Him.

"Don't hold on to Me," Jesus said. "I haven't yet gone up to My Father. Go and tell My disciples this: I'm going up to heaven to My Father and your Father. I'm going to My God and your God."

Mary Magdalene went and told the disciples, "I've seen the Lord!"

303
On the Road to Emmaus
LUKE 24:13–27

Later that day, two disciples were walking from Jerusalem to a town called Emmaus. They were talking about what Mary had told them. A man came and walked with them. The man was Jesus, but they didn't recognize Him! "What are you talking about?" He asked.

"Haven't you heard about Jesus?" they asked Him. "He was a mighty prophet who was just crucified. But an angel told two women that He's alive! They went to His tomb, and it was empty."

"Don't you know that this had to happen to Him?" the man asked. Then He explained the writings of Moses and the prophets to them. He showed them what the scriptures said about Christ.

304
Jesus Appears to His Disciples Part One
LUKE 24:28–37

The two disciples didn't realize that the man walking with them was Jesus. In Emmaus, they sat down to eat together. Jesus picked up some bread, blessed it, and broke it. When He gave the bread to them, they recognized who He was. But then Jesus vanished!

The men rushed back to Jerusalem and told the other disciples, "When He walked with us and explained the scriptures, it felt exciting. It was like a fire burning inside us."

The other disciples said, "Jesus has appeared to Peter too!" And then Jesus Himself stood before them. "Peace be with you," He said.

The disciples thought they were seeing a ghost, and they were afraid.

305
Jesus Appears to His Disciples Part Two
LUKE 24:38–49; JOHN 20:24–28

Jesus said to His disciples, "Why is there doubt and fear in your hearts? Touch Me and see." The disciples were so happy to be with Jesus again! They couldn't believe their eyes.

Jesus taught them, and they were able to completely understand what Moses and other prophets had written about Him—that He, the Christ, would suffer and die and rise from the dead. The whole world would hear about it.

"Soon I'll send you the Holy Spirit," Jesus told them.

The disciple named Thomas hadn't been there that day. He didn't believe what the other disciples told him. "I'll have to touch Jesus' wounds before I believe," he said.

A few days later, Jesus stood among the disciples again. "Reach out, Thomas," He said. "Touch My hands. Don't doubt. Believe."

Thomas touched Jesus' hands. "My Lord and my God," he said.

306
Breakfast on the Seashore
JOHN 21:1–12

Peter, John, and five other disciples had been fishing in their boat all night, but they'd caught nothing. At daybreak, Jesus stood on the beach. The disciples didn't know it was Him.

"Did you catch any fish?" Jesus called to them. "Cast your net on the right side of the boat. There you'll find some." So the disciples did what He said. Their net filled up with so many fish they couldn't lift it into the boat.

"It's the Lord!" John exclaimed.

When Peter heard this, he jumped overboard into the sea and swam to the beach. There he found a fire with fish and bread cooking on it. The other disciples rowed ashore, dragging the net full of fish.

"Bring some more fish," said Jesus. "Come and have breakfast with Me."

307
"Do You Love Me?"
JOHN 21:15–25

When they finished breakfast, Jesus asked Peter, "Peter, do you love Me more than these?"

"Yes, Lord. You know I love You."

"Then feed My lambs," Jesus told him. He asked Peter the same question a second time. "Do you love Me?"

"Yes, Lord. You know I love You."

"Then tend My sheep," Jesus said. Then, for a third time, Jesus asked Peter, "Do you love Me?"

Peter felt hurt that Jesus needed to ask him so many times. "Lord!" he answered. "You know everything. You know I love You."

Jesus said, "Peter, when you were young, you did whatever you wanted. But when you're old, it will be different. Someone will take you where you don't want to go." He meant Peter would someday die because he served God.

Jesus did so many things. The world can't hold all the books that could be written about Him!

308
Jesus Is Taken into Heaven
ACTS 1:3–11

For forty days, Jesus stayed with the disciples. He told them not to leave Jerusalem but to wait there for God's promise.

"I said this before," Jesus told them, "John baptized with water. But in a few days, you will be baptized with the Holy Spirit. You will receive power when God's Spirit comes upon you. Then you will speak for Me, starting in Jerusalem, then in Judea, Samaria, and to the ends of the earth."

After Jesus said this, He was lifted straight up into the sky. A cloud took Him out of sight. While His disciples looked toward heaven, two men wearing white clothes stood with them. "Men from Galilee," they said, "why are you standing there looking up? Jesus has been taken from you into heaven. But He will come back in the same way you saw Him go."

309
Pentecost! Part One
ACTS 2:1–11

The disciples stayed together and prayed together after Jesus went away in the cloud.

Fifty days after Jesus was crucified, there was a big holiday called Pentecost. At that time, thousands of people visited Jerusalem. The disciples were all together when, suddenly, a sound like a violent wind filled their house. Fire appeared to rest on each of them. Then they were all filled with the Holy Spirit. The Spirit made them able to speak in other languages.

A curious crowd gathered. They were from many different nations. But everyone was able to hear the disciples preach the Gospel—the good news about Jesus—in their own language.

310
Pentecost! Part Two
ACTS 2:14–41

Peter stood up and spoke to the crowd. "Long ago, the prophet Joel wrote: 'In the last days, I'll pour My Spirit on everyone. Then those who call on the Lord's name will be saved.' Jesus did miracles among you, but you killed Him. That was God's plan. This same Jesus, God brought back from death. We have seen Him. He sits now at God's right hand. The Father has given Jesus our promise of the Holy Spirit."

The people asked, "What shall we do?"

"Everyone, turn from your sins, be forgiven, and be baptized in the name of Jesus Christ," Peter said. "You'll be given the Holy Spirit as a gift. This promise is for you, your children, and all who are far away."

Three thousand people believed in Jesus that day, and their sins were forgiven.

311
"I'll Give You What I Have"
ACTS 3:1–8

"Give me money, please," begged a man near the temple who was unable to walk. "I've been like this since I was born."

Peter and John, passing nearby, heard the man's plea. "I have no silver or gold," Peter said to him, "but I'll give you what I have. In the name of Jesus Christ of Nazareth, stand up and walk." Peter took the man's hand and helped him up.

Instantly, the man's feet and ankles became strong. Jumping up, the man went into the temple with Peter and John. He was walking, leaping, and praising God.

312
Peter Speaks to the Crowd
ACTS 3:9–4:4

Peter spoke to a crowd at the temple.

"Pilate wanted to free Jesus, but you wanted the murderer Barabbas freed instead. So you killed Jesus. But God brought Him back from death. We have seen Him.

"You didn't know what you were doing, but the prophets all said this would happen to the Lord.

"Now turn to God so your sins will be forgiven. Better times will come because of Jesus. Someday, God will send Him, your Christ, back again."

The priests and other temple officials were upset that the disciples taught at the temple, and especially that they said, "In Jesus, you will be saved from death." They arrested Peter and John and held them until the next day. Still, because of what Peter told them, five thousand believed in Jesus that day.

313
Jesus' Companions
ACTS 4:5–21

The high priests and other leaders asked Peter and John, "In whose name did you heal the disabled beggar?"

Peter, filled with the Holy Spirit, spoke up again. "He was healed by the name of Jesus Christ of Nazareth—the man you crucified and God brought back from death. He is the only One who can save you."

The priests and leaders were amazed by the bold way Peter spoke. He and John were common, uneducated men.

They knew Peter and John had been Jesus' companions. "What should we do with these men?" they asked one another. "Everyone in Jerusalem has heard of this miracle. We can't say it didn't happen." So they ordered the disciples, "Never speak again in the name of Jesus."

"We won't stop speaking about the things we've seen and heard," they said.

314
"You Lied to God!"
ACTS 4:32–5:11

The disciples all stood together, telling anyone who would listen that Jesus was the Christ and that He had been dead and after three days rose from death.

Many of Jesus' followers sold what they had and gave the money to those in need. But a man, Ananias, sold only some of his property. His wife, Sapphira, told him to lie and say he had sold it all. They selfishly kept the remaining money for themselves.

"Ananias," said Peter, "why has Satan caused you to lie? The Holy Spirit knows you held back part of the money. When you lied, you lied to God!"

After hearing what Peter said, both Ananias and Sapphira fell to the ground. When the people heard about this, they were afraid of God's mighty power.

315
Arrested Again
ACTS 5:14–26

Many people believed what the disciples were saying. They carried the sick into the streets of Jerusalem. They believed that if only Peter's shadow fell on the sick people as he passed by, they would be healed. Sick people came from the surrounding cities, and they were healed.

The priests arrested the disciples and put them into prison. But during the night, an angel opened the prison doors. "Go," said the angel. "Stand in the temple and preach."

In the morning, the priests called for the prisoners to be brought to them. "We found the prison locked," their men reported. "The guards were standing at the doors. But no one was inside." Then another report came: "The men you put in prison are teaching in the temple!"

The temple police arrested and brought the apostles to the high priest. Now the temple police were afraid of being punished.

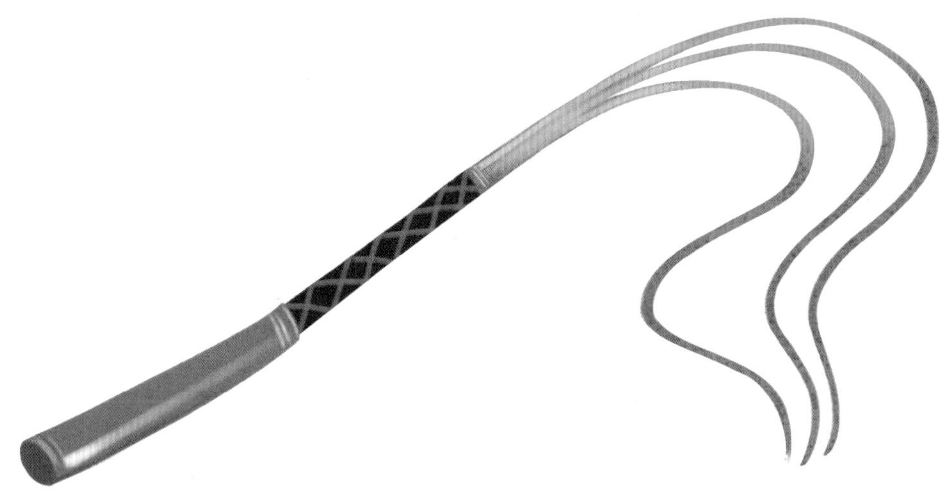

316
"Jesus Is the Christ"
ACTS 5:27–42

"We gave you clear orders!" said the high priest to the disciples. "Don't teach in Jesus' name. Yet you've filled Jerusalem with your teaching."

"We must obey God instead of any human," Peter replied. "You killed Jesus, but God brought Him back from death. Jesus is at God's side now as our Leader and Savior. He wants to give Israel forgiveness of sins. We simply speak the truth."

The leaders were angry, and they wanted the disciples killed. Then a man named Gamaliel spoke up. "I say leave them alone. If their work is human, it will fail. But if it comes from God, you can't stop them. In fact, you may be fighting against God."

The apostles were whipped, ordered not to speak in Jesus' name, and then released. "We are worthy to suffer for His name!" they said—and they never stopped sharing out loud, "Jesus is the Christ!"

317
Stephen, a Faithful Man
Part One
ACTS 6:1–7:1

Jesus' followers kept spreading the good news of the Gospel. Seven men were chosen to care for the sharing of food among believers. One was Stephen, a man of faith. Filled with the Holy Spirit, he performed great miracles. He was so wise that no one could win an argument against him. This made some people angry. They paid to have Stephen accused of a crime he didn't do.

"We've heard Stephen say terrible things against Moses and God," someone said. "He says Jesus of Nazareth will destroy the temple," said another. "He wants to change the traditions Moses gave us."

The high priest looked at Stephen. "Are these things true?" he asked. When he looked at Stephen's face, he saw that it was like the face of an angel.

318
Stephen, a Faithful Man Part Two
ACTS 7:2–60

The high priest and those judging Stephen listened impatiently while Stephen spoke about the history of the Jewish people—beginning with Abraham. "Your ancestors turned against every prophet," Stephen told them. "Those prophets predicted that Christ Jesus would come—and now you're His murderers."

This made his judges so angry that they got up and rushed toward Stephen.

"Look!" Stephen cried. "The heavens are opened. There's Jesus standing next to God."

The men dragged Stephen out of Jerusalem. They threw stones at him again and again. Stephen kneeled and said a prayer like the one Jesus prayed when He was on the cross. "Lord Jesus, receive my spirit," said Stephen. "Don't hold this sin against them."

Then Stephen died.

319
Saul, Jesus' Enemy
ACTS 9:1–5

A young man named Saul was happy when Stephen died. Saul hated people who believed in Jesus. He helped chase Jesus' followers out of Jerusalem, and he threatened to kill Jesus' disciples. He made sure some of the believers were put in jail.

One day Saul went to the nearby city of Damascus. He planned to arrest any Jesus followers who lived there.

While Saul walked on the road toward Damascus, a bright light from heaven flashed all around him. He fell to the ground.

A voice said, "Saul, Saul, why do you treat Me so badly?"

"Who are You?" asked Saul.

The voice answered, "I'm Jesus."

320
Saul, the Believer
ACTS 9:6–19

Saul fell down. He was blinded by the light. "Get up and go into the city. There you'll be told what to do," the voice told him. Some men traveling with Saul led him into Damascus. For three days, Saul was blind and wouldn't eat.

Jesus said to His follower Ananias, "Find Saul and touch him so he can see again."

"Lord," Ananias said, "I've heard of this man. He's done bad things to Your followers."

"Go, Ananias," said Jesus. "I've chosen Saul to bring My name to people of all nations, even to kings and the people of Israel. I will teach him how to suffer. This suffering will be for My name."

So Ananias went. "Saul," he said, "the Lord Jesus has sent me. Receive your sight. Be filled with the Holy Spirit." Instantly, Saul could see again. He was baptized, ate a meal, and got his strength back.

321

Saul, the Preacher

ACTS 9:20–30

Saul stayed for several days with the disciples in Damascus. He went into the Jewish synagogues and said, "Jesus is the Son of God." When those who hated Jesus saw that Saul had turned against them, they made a plan to kill him. But the disciples helped Saul escape by putting him into a basket and lowering it through a hole in the city wall.

When he returned to Jerusalem, Saul tried to join the disciples there.

"He doesn't believe in Jesus," they said.

But a disciple named Barnabas told them how Saul had seen the Lord. "The Lord spoke to him in Damascus," said Barnabas. "And Saul bravely preached the Gospel there."

The disciples in Jerusalem accepted Saul, but his enemies still plotted to kill him. So the believers put Saul on a sailing ship. And Saul sailed home to a place called Tarsus.

322
"Tabitha Is Alive!"
ACTS 9:36–43

Peter traveled from city to city telling people about Jesus. In a place called Joppa, he met Tabitha. She was a Jesus follower who was busy doing good things to help other people.

One day, two men came running to Peter. "Please, come with us. Hurry! Tabitha got sick. She died!"

When Peter got to Tabitha's house, her friends and family were there crying. Peter sent them outside. Then he got on his knees and prayed. Finishing his prayer, Peter said, "Tabitha, get up."

The woman opened her eyes and sat up.

The news spread quickly. "Tabitha is alive!" Many believed in Jesus that day because of what Peter had done.

323
A Vision from the Lord
ACTS 10:1–23

Cornelius was a Roman soldier. He was a Gentile—not a Jew—yet he was true to God, gave to the poor, and always prayed. One day, Cornelius saw an angel!

"Cornelius," the angel said, "send men to Joppa and find Peter at Simon's house." So Cornelius sent for Peter.

Meanwhile, at Simon's house, Peter saw a vision from the Lord. A large sheet filled with all kinds of animals came down from heaven. A voice said, "Peter, you may eat the meat of these beasts."

But all the animals in the sheet were banned by Jewish law. There were only certain kinds of meat that were considered "clean," meaning they were okay to eat.

"No, Lord," said Peter. "I've never eaten any unclean meat."

"God has made this meat clean," said the voice. "You may eat it from now on."

Just then, the men arrived and invited Peter to Cornelius's house.

324
The Spirit and the Gentiles
ACTS 10:24–48

Cornelius kneeled to worship Peter when he and several other disciples arrived. "Get up," Peter said. "It's wrong to worship a man."

It was wrong for a Jew to visit a Gentile too, but Peter believed God had led him there. "Why have you sent for me?" he asked.

"An angel came to me," said Cornelius. "He told me, 'God has heard your prayers. Send men to Joppa and find Peter.' I did this, and you're kind enough to come. We're here in the presence of God to listen to you."

So Peter began sharing with Cornelius and his friends and family the good news about Jesus and forgiveness of sins. Suddenly, the Holy Spirit came down on all those listening to him. Peter was amazed! The Father's gift of the Holy Spirit had been poured into the Gentiles!

"Let's baptize these people in the name of Jesus Christ," said Peter.

325
The Lord Rescues Peter
ACTS 12:1–11

The evil King Herod was still at work trying to stop anyone who followed the way of Jesus. He had already killed one of the disciples, James, and then he had Peter arrested and put in prison.

When the church—all those who followed Jesus—found out, they got busy praying.

While Peter sat in prison, he couldn't believe his eyes when he saw an angel come into his cell!

"Get up quickly, Peter. Put on your sandals," the angel said.

Peter did as he was told.

"Now, follow me."

Peter walked with the angel past the prison guards, who did not see them. The prison gate swung open all by itself, and the angel led Peter down a narrow city street. Then the angel disappeared.

"The Lord has rescued me," Peter said.

326
Peter and the Prayer Meeting
ACTS 12:12–17

After escaping prison, Peter went to his friend Mary's house and knocked on the door. Believers were gathered at her house, praying for Peter to be released from prison. Mary's maid went to the door. "Who is it?" she asked. When she heard Peter's voice, she was so excited she forgot to open the door to let Peter in. Instead, she ran to tell the others.

Meanwhile, Peter continued knocking. When they opened the door, they were amazed. At first, they thought Peter had died and this was his spirit.

"Quiet, quiet," Peter whispered, worried that the prison guards might be after him. Then he described how an angel had helped him escape. "Tell this to the believers," he said. Then Peter went to another place.

327
A New Name: Christians
ACTS 11:19–30

Before long, there were Jesus followers all over the Middle East. A great number of them were Gentiles.

When the Jewish believers in Jerusalem heard that many Greeks in Antioch had turned to Jesus, they sent Barnabas to speak with them. He was a good man, full of the Holy Spirit. "Be faithful to the Lord," he told the people there. "Stay close to Him."

Then Barnabas went to Tarsus to find Saul. He found him and brought him back to Antioch. They spent the next year together in Antioch, teaching the Gentile believers there. These people were not at all like Jews, and they had also changed in ways that made them different from Gentiles. So it was in Antioch that a new name was given to Jesus' followers. They were called "Christians."

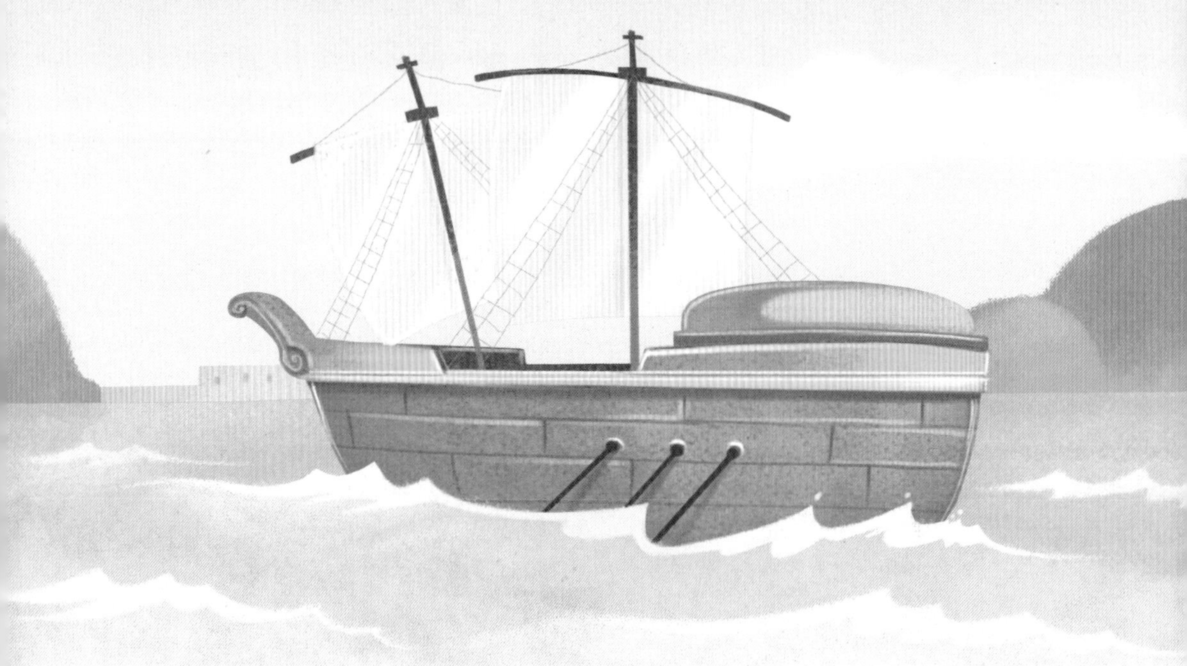

328
The Man Named Paul
ACTS 13:1–12

Saul had taken a new name. He called himself Paul. He, Barnabas, and another disciple, John Mark, sailed to the island of Cyprus. They taught God's Word to the people there.

On the island, they found many false prophets—men telling lies that their words came from God. One, a magician named Bar-Jesus, tried to keep the ruler of Cyprus from accepting Jesus as Lord. When Paul saw this, he said to the magician, "You are the enemy of all that's right. Stop making the Lord's straight paths crooked! God is against you. You'll be blind for a while."

Then the magician could only see darkness. Someone had to hold his hand and lead him around. When Cyprus's ruler saw this, he believed Jesus is the Christ. He was delighted to hear Paul's teaching about the Lord.

This was the first of many trips Paul made to share the news about Jesus.

329
A Light for the Gentiles
ACTS 13:13–52

Paul and Barnabas returned to Antioch. Huge crowds gathered to hear them speak about how the words of ancient prophets had come true. They said Jesus was the Christ and He had come back from death.

Some of the Jews insisted that Paul and Barnabas were lying.

"God wanted His word to come to you—the Jews—first," said Paul. "But you don't seem to think you're worthy of eternal life. So we're going to tell the Gentiles. God commanded us to do this. He said, 'You are to be a light for the Gentiles. Then you can bring My salvation to the ends of the earth.' "

When the Gentiles heard this, they were glad. They praised God's word and shared it with others. The Jews didn't like this. They sent Paul and Barnabas away. The men left gladly, shaking Antioch's dust from their feet.

330
“The Gods Have Come to Us!”
ACTS 14:1–19

Next, Paul and Barnabas went to a place called Lystra.

Paul healed a man who could not walk. “Stand up on your feet!” he said. The man stood and walked. The crowds saw this. Many were nonbelievers.

“The gods have come to us as men!” they exclaimed. “This one”—they pointed at Barnabas—“is Zeus. The other man is Hermes!” (Zeus and Hermes were the names given to two fake gods.) Then the priests brought oxen to them as offerings.

“Friends!” Paul and Barnabas shouted. “Why are you doing this? We're human, just like you. We've brought good news: Turn from these worthless things! The living God made heaven and earth and everything in them. He fills your hearts with joy!”

Some of Paul's enemies from Antioch had traveled to Lystra. They turned the crowd against Paul. They threw stones at him and dragged him out of the city.

331
"We're Saved through Grace"
ACTS 15:1–21

God had opened the door of faith for the Gentiles! But some of the Jews told them, "You must also keep Moses' law."

Paul and Barnabas said to them, "God is happy that the Gentiles have believed in Jesus. They don't have to do anything else to be saved." Then they went to Jerusalem to discuss this important problem with other disciples.

Peter spoke first. "God gave the Gentiles the Holy Spirit. I was at Cornelius's house when it happened. So God must not see a difference between them and us. Anyway, no one has ever been able to keep Moses' law. We're saved through the grace of the Lord Jesus Christ. So are the Gentiles."

Paul and Barnabas then told of the miracles God did among the Gentiles.

James had the final word: "God wants to make the Gentiles into a people for His name. Let's not trouble them."

332
Paul and Lydia
ACTS 15:40–16:1–15

Paul and another disciple, Silas, helped the new Jesus followers grow stronger in their faith. In Lystra, Paul met a young follower named Timothy. The men began traveling together, sharing the news about Jesus.

One night, Paul had a vision of a man who lived in Macedonia, across the sea in Europe. The man begged, "Come help us!" Paul believed God was telling him to sail to Europe and preach the good news there. So, along with Timothy, Silas, and the disciple Luke, Paul sailed to Europe.

In Macedonia, they traveled to a riverside where they found some women. One woman, Lydia, had a business selling purple cloth. She believed in the one true God. Paul and his friends baptized Lydia and everyone who lived with her. Then she invited the men to stay at her house for a while.

333
Paul and the Fortune-Teller
ACTS 16:16–28

Luke wrote about Paul's travels:

We met a slave girl controlled by a spirit. She worked as a fortune-teller, and her owners took any money she made. The girl annoyed Paul, following him, until he said to the spirit, "I order you in Jesus' name. Come out of her!" And it did. Then she stopped telling fortunes, and her owners made no money.

They took Paul and Silas to the city's leaders, who beat them and locked them in a deep, dark prison cell.

At midnight, Paul and Silas were praying and singing hymns. Suddenly, a violent earthquake shook the prison. The doors opened, and the prisoners' chains fell off. When the jailer saw the prison open, he grabbed his sword. He was about to kill himself—worried he would be killed anyway for allowing his prisoners to escape. But Paul shouted, "Don't hurt yourself! We're all here."

334
Paul, Silas, and the Jailer
ACTS 16:29–40

Luke continued his story:

The jailer rushed into the prison cell. He fell down trembling in front of Paul and Silas. "What do I have to do to be saved?" he asked.

They told him, "Believe in the Lord Jesus and you will be saved with your household." They went with the jailer to his house. There they spoke God's word to him and his family. The jailer was kind to them and washed their wounds. He welcomed Paul and Silas to baptize him and his family, and they all sat down to a meal together to celebrate. They had become believers in Jesus!

Afterward, Paul and Silas returned to Lydia's home, and they kept encouraging the new believers there.

335
Many Believe
ACTS 17:1–15

Paul and his friends traveled to a place called Thessalonica, and Paul taught in the synagogue there. He explained why Christ had to die, and he proved that Christ had to come back from death. "The Christ is Jesus," said Paul. "He's the man I'm telling you about."

Many people there—Jews, Greeks, both men and women—became believers because of Paul, Timothy, and Silas. But some of the Jews caused trouble. They shouted, "These people have been turning the world upside down. Now they've come to our city!"

So Paul and the others went to nearby Berea, where the Jews were kind to them. Many of them became believers there until the troublemakers from Thessalonica showed up. They began turning people against Paul. Afraid for his life, he hurried away to Athens. Later, Timothy and Silas would join him there.

336
Paul, the Babbler Part One
ACTS 17:16–25

In the city of Athens, Paul was known as a babbler—a person who talks too much. He talked all the time about Jesus. Some of the people there did nothing but talk about new ideas. "We'd like to know more about this strange idea of Jesus Christ," they said.

So Paul told them, "There is an interesting altar in your city. On it is written TO AN UNKNOWN GOD. The God of Jesus Christ is the only God. He made the world and everything in it. He is the Lord of heaven and earth. He has no need of anything humans can give. Instead, He gives us life and breath and all things."

337
Paul, the Babbler Part Two
ACTS 17:26–34

Paul continued:

"From one ancestor, God made all the different races. He decided when and where on earth they would live. He is not far from each of us. We are His children. And since we are His children, how can God be a made-up stone image?"

The people listened carefully to Paul's words.

"God wants everyone to turn from fake gods and worship Him. A day has been set when the world will be judged. God has chosen a man to be the judge. He's brought Him back from death."

Someone interrupted Paul, laughing. "A man brought back from death?" A few in the crowd laughed with him, but others joined Paul and believed.

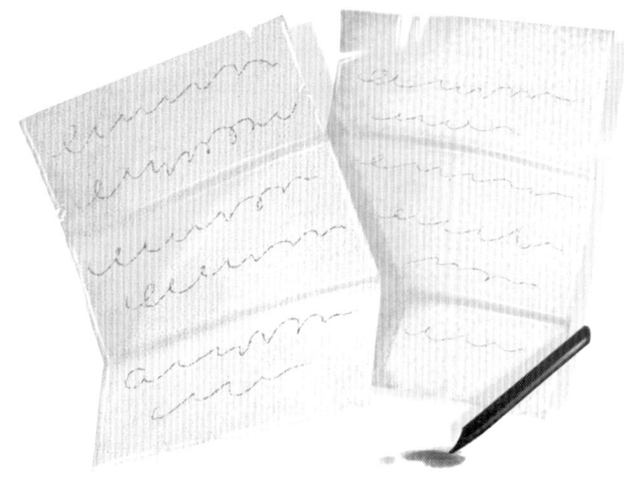

338
Paul Goes to Corinth
ACTS 18:1–11

Paul traveled to Corinth, where he worked making tents with a man named Aquila and his wife, Priscilla. Paul kept trying to convince the Jews that Jesus was the Christ, but they only argued with him. Finally, Paul shook the dust from his coat into their faces and said, "This means I'm done with you. You'll answer to God for refusing the truth. I'm going to pay attention to the Gentiles."

But God spoke to Paul: "Don't be afraid. Keep speaking to them. I'm with you, and no one will harm you. Many people in Corinth belong to Me."

So Paul stayed in Corinth, working like a farmer among the people by planting the seeds of God's Word in their hearts. While there, he wrote two letters to the believers in Thessalonica. He wanted them to live a holy, hardworking life. "Look forward to the day Jesus comes again," he wrote.

339
Paul Goes to Ephesus
ACTS 19:1–17

Paul's third long journey took him from Antioch to Ephesus. Everyone living in Asia had heard the Lord's word. The Jews heard the truth, and so did the Greeks. God did amazing miracles through Paul, including healing the sick.

There were people in Ephesus who pretended they were healers. They tried using the name of the Lord Jesus, like Paul had done. Seven of these healers spoke to a man with an evil spirit living inside him. They commanded it to leave, saying, "I command you by the Jesus that Paul preaches!"

The spirit answered, "I know Jesus. I know Paul too. But who are you?" Then the man with the evil spirit jumped onto them. He beat them badly. Everyone in Ephesus heard of this. They were amazed by the power of Jesus.

340
The Goddess of Ephesus Part One
ACTS 19:18–31

Some of the magicians in Ephesus became believers and burned their magic books in public. Those who worshipped fake gods were worried. The temple of an idol named Diana was a big deal in Ephesus. A silversmith named Demetrius made and sold little shrines honoring the goddess. He said to his workers, "We get all our money from this business. But Paul says handmade gods aren't gods! Many people are believing him. Our business could be ruined. If this goes further, the temple of the great goddess Diana might be destroyed."

"Great is Diana of the Ephesians!" they shouted.

Soon, the city of Ephesus was filled with confusion. A huge crowd hurried to gather in the city's outdoor theater. Paul wanted to go inside with the crowd, but some of his followers warned him, "Don't go in!"

341
The Goddess of Ephesus Part Two
ACTS 19:32–20:6

The theater was filled with shouting people. A man named Alexander quieted them. When they found out he was a Jew, they shouted, "He doesn't worship Diana! Great is Diana of the Ephesians!"

Finally, the town clerk took control. "Citizens of Ephesus!" he shouted. "Everyone knows that our city keeps the temple of Diana. Her statue, which fell to us from heaven, is here. No one can say this isn't true. So you should be quiet. Don't become violent. These men haven't robbed the temple, nor have they cursed the goddess." Then he told the silversmiths to take their problem to court, and he sent the people home.

After the uproar was over, Paul met with the Ephesian believers. He encouraged them to keep telling the people about Jesus. Then he said goodbye to them and left for Macedonia. From there, Paul and his companions traveled to Troas.

342
Paul Talks; Eutychus Sleeps
ACTS 20:6–17

Paul kept traveling, spreading the good news about Jesus wherever he went. The night before he left on another trip, Paul met with his friends to share a meal and talk. After dark, many lamps lit the upstairs meeting room. Paul was talking past midnight.

A young man named Eutychus fell asleep. He was sitting in an open window, and suddenly he crashed to the ground three floors below! Someone shouted, "He's dead!" Paul went down, picked him up, and said, "Don't worry. His life is still in him." Eutychus went away alive, and everyone was happy. They continued talking until dawn.

Paul sailed down the coast of Asia and then decided to return to Jerusalem for Pentecost. On the way, he sent a message to Ephesus: "I'm coming to visit you!" Soon his friends there were hurrying to greet him.

343
Paul's Farewell
ACTS 20:18–38

Paul had a short visit with his friends from Ephesus.

"The Holy Spirit is leading me to Jerusalem," he told them. "I know hardship and prison await me there, and I might even die. I just want to finish my work. This is the important thing: to declare the good news of God's grace.

"After today, you will never see me again. I've told you about God's purpose. Now the rest is up to you. I hand you over to God and the message of His grace.

"I have never asked for money. Instead, I worked with these two hands for myself and my friends. Remember the Lord's words: 'It's more blessed to give than to receive.' "

When Paul finished speaking, they all cried and kneeled to pray. It was the last time they would be together.

344
On the Way to Jerusalem
ACTS 21:1–14

Paul, Luke, and other followers sailed on toward Jerusalem. Luke told what happened next:

"At the city of Tyre, believers warned us not to go to Jerusalem. Before we left there, everyone followed us out of the city. We kneeled on the beach, prayed, and said goodbye.

"We sailed on to Caesarea. While we were there, a man named Agabus tied himself up with Paul's belt. 'These are the Holy Spirit's words,' he said. 'The Jews in Jerusalem will tie up the owner of this belt. They will give him to the Gentiles.' Then everyone urged Paul not to go to Jerusalem. They begged him and cried.

" 'Your weeping is breaking my heart," Paul told them. "I'm ready to die in Jerusalem for the Lord's name.'

"Nothing more was said except, 'Let the Lord do what He wants.' "

345
Paul Enters the Temple
ACTS 21:15–27

Luke continued:

"In Jerusalem, Paul visited James and others. He told them of God's work with the Gentiles. James said, 'Some Jews here follow Moses' law. They falsely believe you want to throw it out. These people will soon know you're here. Four men are going to take a vow in the temple. Go with them and pay their fees. Then everyone will know you care for Moses' law.' Paul knew the Jews could keep the law if they wanted, and the Gentiles didn't need to keep the law. Either way, God wants people to trust His grace and believe in Jesus.

So Paul and the men entered the temple. Paul didn't do this to make God happy. He just wanted people to stop lying about him. But in the temple were men who had hated Paul in Asia. When they saw Paul, they said, "Here's our chance to get him."

346
Paul Is Dragged from the Temple
ACTS 21:28–22:1

"Israelites, help!" the men who hated Paul shouted. "This is the man who is against Moses' law and this temple. Look! He's brought Gentiles here and made this holy place filthy!"

The people ran to Paul and dragged him from the temple.

When Roman soldiers saw the mob, they rescued Paul. There was such an uproar that their captain couldn't hear. "Who is this man?" he asked. "What has he done?"

"Away with him!" shouted the crowd. So the soldiers arrested Paul in chains and carried him away.

Paul begged the captain. "I'm a Jew, a citizen of Tarsus. Please let me speak to the people." So the captain gave his permission.

Paul signaled the crowd to be silent. "Friends," he began, "listen to what I have to say."

347
Paul Speaks to the Crowd
ACTS 22:2–22

Paul continued:

"I'm a Jew, born in Tarsus. I used to hate Christians. I was on my way to Damascus to arrest Christians when a great light from heaven flashed. I fell to the ground, and a voice said, 'Saul, Saul, why are you against Me?'

" 'Who are You?' I asked.

" 'I'm Jesus of Nazareth.'

"In Damascus, a good Jewish man named Ananias met me. 'God has chosen you,' he said. 'You will tell the world of what you've seen and heard. Now get up and be baptized in Jesus' name.'

"Then I came here to Jerusalem and was praying in the temple when the Lord appeared. 'Get out of this city,' He said. 'The people won't listen to you. Go; I am sending you far away to the Gentiles.' "

When they heard the word *Gentiles*, the crowd shouted in anger.

348
Saved from the Angry Crowd
ACTS 22:22–30

"Away with him!" the people shouted. "He shouldn't be allowed to live." They threw off their coats and tossed dust into the air.

The captain hurried Paul into the building. They were about to whip him when Paul said, "This is against Roman law. I'm a citizen, and I've done nothing wrong."

The soldiers were afraid when they heard this. They'd chained a Roman citizen. The captain didn't know what Paul had done to make the people angry. So he brought him to the priests and the Jewish council.

349
Saved from the Jewish Council
ACTS 23:1–11

Facing the council, Paul said, "Brothers, I've always lived for God—"

"Hit him!" the high priest ordered.

"You pretend to judge me by the law. But hitting me breaks the law," said Paul.

"Do you dare put down God's high priest?" someone asked.

"I didn't know he was the high priest," Paul replied. "The scriptures say, 'Don't speak evil of your leaders.' I'm on trial because of one thing: the hope of the resurrection of the dead."

When they heard this, some of the men wanted to let Paul go. Others refused. The Roman captain thought, *They're going to kill him.* So the soldiers rescued Paul again, dragging him away from the angry men.

That night, the Lord came to Paul and said, "Be brave. You've spoken for Me here. You will speak for Me in Rome too."

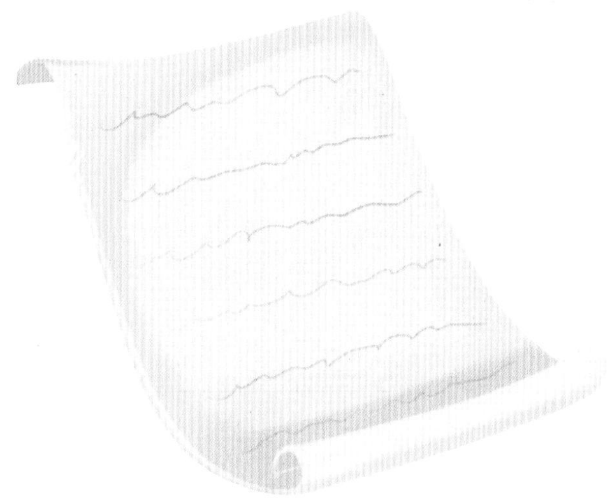

350
Paul and 470 Soldiers
ACTS 23:12–35

Those who hated Paul planned to kill him. They went to the council and told them their plans. "Call for Paul to come back for another meeting. We'll kill him before he gets here," they said.

When Paul's nephew heard about the plan, he went secretly to tell the captain.

The captain ordered his men, "Get ready to leave by nine o'clock tonight. Take our prisoner, Paul, to Caesarea. Call together two hundred soldiers, seventy horsemen, and two hundred spearmen. Provide a horse for Paul, and bring him to Felix, the governor." The captain wrote a letter to Felix explaining the situation. Then he told those who planned to kill Paul, "Go to the governor with your problem."

That night, Paul and 470 Roman soldiers left Jerusalem. At Caesarea, they delivered the letter and Paul to the governor.

"I'll hear your case. But not until your accusers get here," Felix said.

351
Paul Speaks to Felix Part One
ACTS 24:1–16

The high priest and other temple leaders came with their lawyer to the governor in Caesarea. The lawyer told Felix, "Paul is a pest in our nation. He stirs up Jews all over the world. He even tried to infect the temple with Gentiles. We wanted to judge him ourselves. But the captain took him away from us. That's why we're here today."

Then Paul said to Felix, "This is my side of the story. I went to worship in Jerusalem. I didn't argue with anyone or stir up the crowds. They can't prove the things they say against me. I worship the same God as my ancestors, the Israelites. I believe in the law and the prophets. My hope in God is the same as theirs. I always do my best to have a good heart, free from wrong before God and before people."

352

Paul Speaks to Felix Part Two

ACTS 24:17–27

Paul continued speaking to the governor:

"I came to Jerusalem, bringing gifts for the poor. I went to the temple to give an offering, and my enemies from Asia were there. They're the ones who should be here today. They have something against me. These men here should tell you I was brought to their council. There I mentioned that God would bring us back from death. Maybe that upset them."

Felix knew quite a bit about the Christian way. "The Roman captain must come here," he said. "Then I'll decide this matter."

While waiting for the captain, Paul explained the Gospel of Jesus to Felix and his wife. Paul talked about God's judgment. These things frightened Felix. "Go away for now," he told Paul. "I'll send for you again when I can."

Paul waited there in prison for two years.

353
Paul and the New Governor
ACTS 24:27–25:12

A new governor, Festus, came to power. He kept Paul in prison. The priests and leaders in Jerusalem sent a message to Festus: "Send Paul here. We'll settle this problem." But their real plan was to attack Paul and kill him.

"No," said Festus. "You come to me."

"I've done nothing against the Jewish law," Paul told the new governor. "I didn't disrespect the temple, and I always respect the Roman emperor."

Festus said, "Do you want to go to Jerusalem to settle this?"

Paul knew he'd be killed if he went back there. "I've done no wrong to the Jews," he said. "I'm not trying to escape. I've done nothing that deserves death. So why would you turn me over to them? Instead, I'd like to take my case to the emperor in Rome."

"You want the emperor to hear your case?" asked Festus. "Then I will send you there."

354
The King Hears the Gospel Part One
ACTS 25:13–26:19

King Agrippa of Galilee and his wife came to visit Festus. "I'd like to speak with Paul," said the king. So Festus had Paul brought to him.

"You have my permission to speak," said the king.

"I'm glad to tell you my story, King Agrippa," Paul began. "You know the Jewish customs and law. Please listen patiently. I'm on trial because I believe God's promise to our ancestors. All the Jews hope for this as well. It is that God will bring us back from death. Yet now they accuse me because I believe this!

"I hated the name of Jesus. I was furious and punished Christians. I even traveled to faraway places to arrest them." Then Paul described what had happened to him at Damascus and how he came to believe in the Lord.

355
The King Hears the Gospel Part Two
ACTS 26:20–32

Paul continued speaking to King Agrippa:

"Everywhere I went, I said to people, 'Change your mind! Turn to God!' I told both Jews and Gentiles. That's why the Jews tried to kill me. But God has helped me. My message is the same as Moses' and the prophets': Christ would suffer; He would be first to return from death; He would give light to all people."

"You're out of your mind, Paul!" exclaimed Festus.

"I tell you the truth," Paul answered.

"Do you want me to be a Christian?" asked the king.

"I want you all to be like me," said Paul, "—except without these chains."

356
Paul's Dangerous Voyage Part One
ACTS 26:30–27:11

"Paul has done nothing wrong," said King Agrippa. "He could have been set free. But now he has to take his case to the emperor."

So Paul was sent traveling to Rome, put on a sailing ship with other prisoners and a Roman soldier, Julius, in charge. They sailed along the coast of Judea, and on the way, they docked in Sidon, where Paul was allowed to visit his friends.

Sailing became slow. The wind blew the wrong direction, and the ship took much longer than planned to get to the island of Crete. Winter would have to pass before they could sail on to Italy.

Paul spoke to the ship's captain and owner: "I can see that this will be a dangerous voyage. The cargo will be lost, and so will our lives."

But they paid no attention to what Paul said.

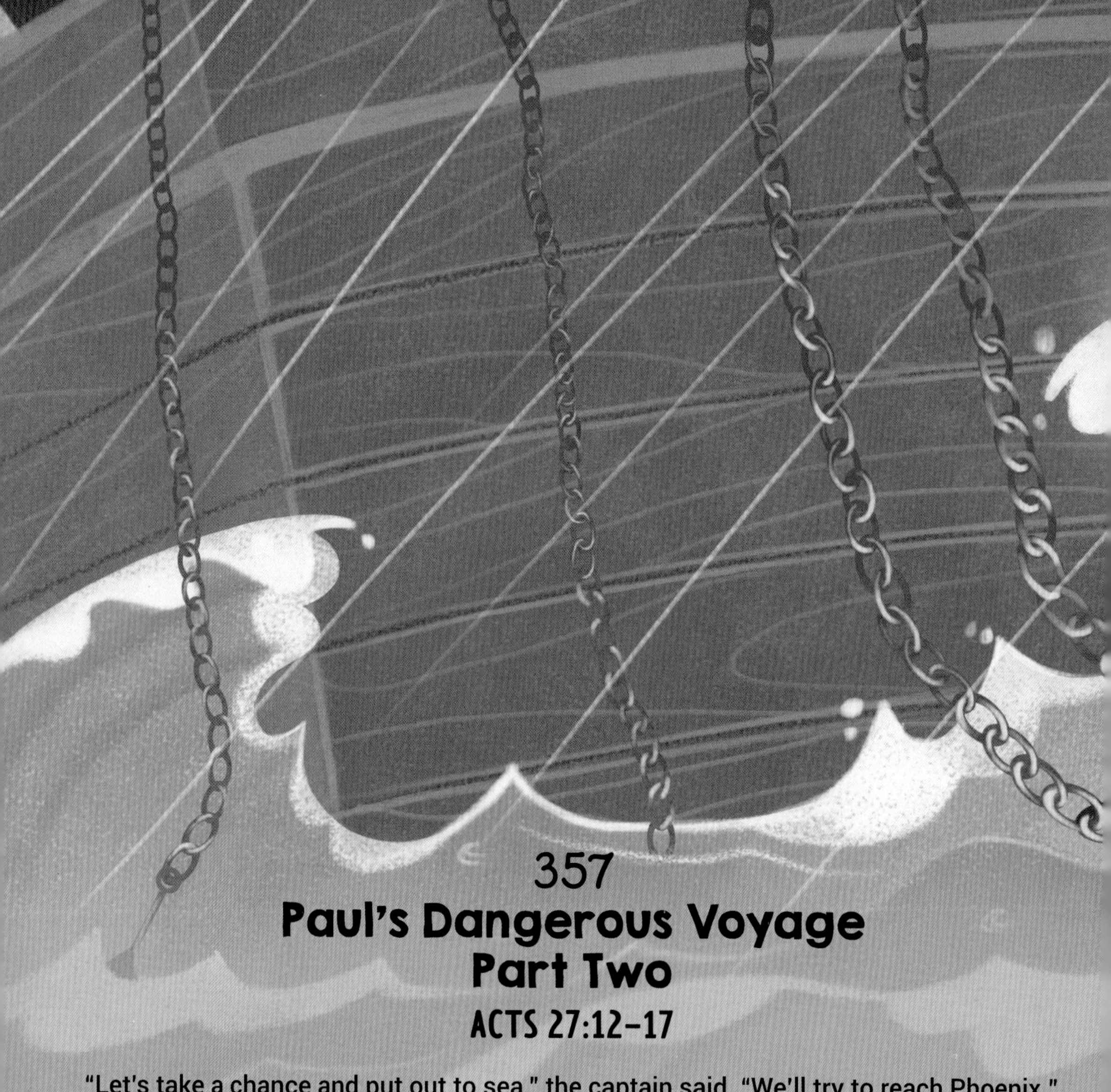

357
Paul's Dangerous Voyage Part Two

ACTS 27:12–17

"Let's take a chance and put out to sea," the captain said. "We'll try to reach Phoenix."

The nearby harbor would be safe from the winter storms. They pulled up the anchor and set sail, trying to stay close to shore. But a wild wind rushed at them from the northeast. It drove the ship far from shore. They lost sight of land, and the men saw only sea and sky. Struggling for control, the crew lowered the anchor.

358
Paul's Dangerous Voyage Part Three
ACTS 27:18–32

Powerful waves pounded the ship. The men threw tools, equipment, and cargo overboard. The sailors lost all hope they would survive.

Paul shouted to them: "Last night, an angel stood by me. He said, 'Don't be afraid, Paul. You must speak to the Roman emperor. God has granted safety to those who are sailing with you.' So, men, keep up your courage. I have faith in my God. It will be just as He said."

The storm finally calmed. For two weeks, the ship drifted along. Then, late one night, the water became shallow because they were near land. Someone said, "We'll crash onto the rocks!" So they dropped anchor and prayed for daylight.

The sailors planned to leave the ship and swim to shore. But Paul told Julius, "Tell them to stay; otherwise, no one will be saved."

The soldier listened to him. And the men stayed.

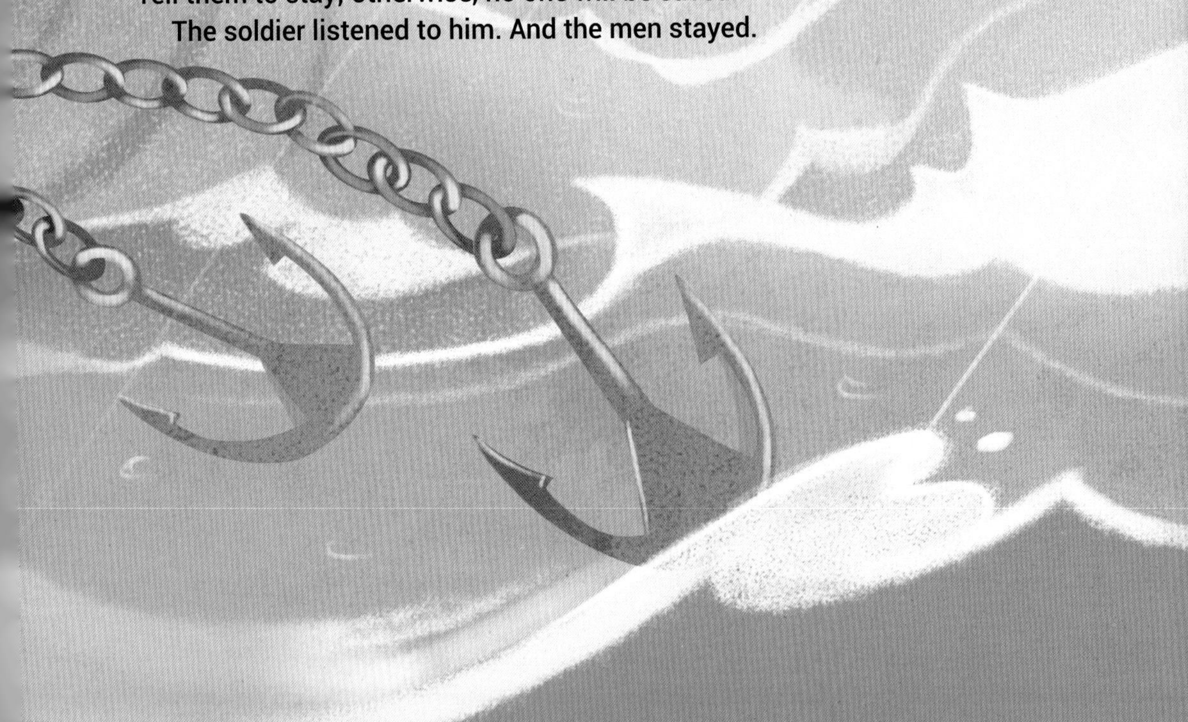

359
Shipwrecked!
ACTS 27:33–44

It was almost dawn. "We haven't eaten for two weeks," said Paul. "Please, have some food. It will help you survive." Everyone watched Paul. He took bread, gave thanks to God, broke it, and began to eat. Then all the other sailors took food. Everyone ate and was satisfied.

In the daylight, they saw land. "Run the ship up on the beach," ordered the captain. The men lifted the anchor. They raised the sail and rowed toward the sand. But then the ship struck an underwater reef and got stuck. Waves came pounding again. They broke the wooden ship apart.

The soldiers said, "Let's kill the prisoners, or they'll escape." But Julius wanted to save Paul, and he wouldn't allow this.

The captain shouted, "If you can swim, jump overboard!" Some did. Others came ashore floating on pieces of wood. Everyone was brought safely to land.

360
Paul Arrives in Rome
ACTS 28:1–23

While shipwrecked on the little island of Malta, the kind people there built a fire to warm the cold, wet survivors. Paul was bringing brushwood to the fire when a snake hiding in the wood bit him. He shook it off into the fire. The islanders were amazed when Paul didn't drop dead of a snakebite. Some thought he was a god.

While on the island, Paul prayed, and through him God healed many sick people who lived there.

Then a new ship carried Paul and the others to Italy. Believers from Rome heard Paul was coming, and they came to greet him.

In Rome, Paul lived in his own house with a guard. The Jewish leaders visited him there. "We've heard bad things about the Christians," they said. "But we'd like to know what you have to say."

361
The Gentiles Will Listen
ACTS 28:23–28

From morning until evening, many Jewish leaders from Rome listened to Paul. As they thought about his words, they were confused and started arguing with one another.

Paul said to them: "The Holy Spirit said to your ancestors, 'They will listen but won't catch My meaning. They will see but won't understand. Your words will do them no good. They won't use their eyes to look. They won't use their ears to hear. They won't understand with their minds. Turn to Me and be healed.' The Holy Spirit was right."

"I want you to know this," he continued. "Through His grace, God rescues us from the punishment of sin—and this salvation has been sent to the Gentiles. They will listen."

362
Paul's Life on Earth Ends
ACTS 28:30; 2 TIMOTHY 4:6–8

Paul waited in prison for two years. The men who accused him in Jerusalem never showed up to speak to the Roman emperor. After he was released from prison, Paul continued traveling, sharing the good news about Jesus and caring for all the churches.

Meanwhile, a huge fire almost destroyed Rome. Christians were being blamed. And although no one really knew what, or who, had started the blaze, this might be why Paul was arrested a second time.

From prison, he wrote to his friend Timothy: "It's now time for me to leave this life. I've fought a good fight. I've finished the race. I've kept the faith. The Lord has a crown waiting for me. He'll give it to me on the day He returns. Everyone who loves Him and His return will get such a crown."

Paul was never released from prison. He died a prisoner.

363
John's Vision of Jesus Christ Part One
REVELATION 1:9–13

When Jesus' disciple John was a very old man, he lived in prison on an island called Patmos. He was the last living disciple who had been with Jesus on earth.

John wrote these words about a vision he had:

Behind me, I heard a loud voice like a trumpet. I turned to look when I heard the voice. There, walking among seven gold lampstands, was Jesus Christ.

The last time John had seen Jesus was sixty years before when Jesus had come back from death.

364
John's Vision of Jesus Christ Part Two
REVELATION 1:13–20

John continued:

Jesus wore a long robe with a golden sash across His chest. His hair was white like snow, His eyes like flaming fire. His feet shone like polished brass, and His voice sounded like rushing streams of water. Seven stars were on His right hand, and His face was like the brightest sun. "Don't be afraid," He told me. "I'm the first and the last. I'm the Living One. I was dead, and look, I am alive forever. Write what I'll show you. Send the book to the seven churches in Asia. These seven stars are the angels of the seven churches. These gold lampstands are the seven churches."

John wrote the book called Revelation. It includes letters to the Christian churches. It also tells of the end of time. It shows us what it will be like to live forever with God.

365
Forever Life with God
REVELATION 21:1–22:21

John wrote in his book:

I saw a new heaven and a new earth. Then Jerusalem came from heaven like a bride arriving for her husband. A loud voice came from God's throne, and it said, "God's home is with all humans. He will live with them; they'll be His people. God will wipe every tear from their eyes. There will be no more death. Grief, crying, and pain will be gone. Old things are gone. He's making everything new."

John described how beautiful New Jerusalem was: colorful stone buildings, streets of gold, and gates made of pearls. He wrote:

The river of the water of life flows from God's throne. The tree of life grows on the riverbanks. Its leaves heal the nations.

Jesus says, "Come. Anyone who wishes may drink this water of life." Jesus says all of this is true. He is coming back someday. Come, Lord Jesus!

Enjoy the Following 3-Minute Bedtime Prayers—

A great way to get a good night's sleep!

From *3-Minute Bedtime Prayers for Little Hearts*

ISBN 978-1-64352-281-4

INTRODUCTION

Everything in the Bible Is True

Open my eyes so that I may see great things from Your Law.
PSALM 119:18

Dear God, thank You for the Bible. It is filled with stories about how You help the people who love You. The Bible's words remind me that You love me and will help me every day, wherever I am. Best of all, the Bible is filled with promises that are for me—right now. So teach me about Your promises, God. I want to learn about them and live my life trusting in each one. Amen.

Think about it!

Why is it important to read the Bible?

GOD MADE ME

God Created Me

"Before I started to put you together in your mother, I knew you. Before you were born, I set you apart as holy. I chose you to speak to the nations for Me."

JEREMIAH 1:5

Dear God, help me to remember that You made me. Before I was born, even before You put my body together, You knew all about me. You planned what I would look like, where I would live, and all the people I would ever meet. You knew my favorite colors and what I would be really good at. Best of all, God, You made me to be Yours, always and forever. Thank You! Amen.

Think about it!

What do you like best about the way God created you?

I Am a Gift from God

See, children are a gift from the Lord.
The children born to us are our special reward.
Psalm 127:3

Dear God, I've never thought of myself as a gift, but You say that's what I am. A gift is something special because it is given with love. When You created me, You made me special. You formed my body exactly the way You wanted it to be. Then You put all Your love into me and gave me to my parents. I am their best gift ever! I love You, God. Amen.

Think about it!

What makes you special?

"The Lord your God has chosen you out of all the nations on the earth, to be His own."
DEUTERONOMY 7:6

Dear God, I feel special when someone chooses me as a friend, and I feel extra special knowing that You chose me to be Yours. You made me so You could love me now and forever. You created me as one of a kind. In the whole world, there is no one just like me. Tonight when I close my eyes to sleep, I will remember that You chose me to be Your own. Good night, God. Amen.

Think about it!

In what ways are you different (and special!) from everyone else?

God Made Me Beautiful

"You are all beautiful, my love. You are perfect."
SONG OF SOLOMON 4:7

Dear God, everything You make is perfect, and that is how You made me. I am Your perfect creation. You made me the way You wanted me to be. And when You finished making me, You looked at me and decided that I was the most beautiful child You had ever seen. You feel that way about me all the time. So help me to remember every day that I am Your beautiful child. Amen.

Think about it!

What is your favorite thing about God's creation?

God Gave Me a Beautiful Heart

Your beauty should come from the inside.
It should come from the heart. This is the kind that lasts. Your beauty should be a gentle and quiet spirit. In God's sight this is of great worth and no amount of money can buy it.

1 Peter 3:4

Dear God, when You created me, You gave special attention to my heart. You made it a beautiful place that You can fill with Your love. You have poured so much love in there that I have plenty left over to share with others. Thank You, dear God, for my beautiful heart! I love You so much. Amen.

Think about it!

What makes someone's heart beautiful?

God's Spirit Lives inside Me

Do you not know that your body is a house of God where the Holy Spirit lives? God gave you His Holy Spirit. Now you belong to God. You do not belong to yourselves. God bought you with a great price. So honor God with your body. You belong to Him.

1 Corinthians 6:19–20

Dear God, I know that You love me and that You are with me all the time. The Bible says that Your Spirit lives inside me. I have trouble imagining that sometimes. But I know that You are God, and that means You can go anywhere and do anything. Remind me to keep my body healthy and clean so it is a nice place for You to live in. Amen.

Think about it!

How does it feel to know you belong to God?

I Am Important to God

"Are not two small birds sold for a very small piece of money? And yet not one of the birds falls to the earth without your Father knowing it. God knows how many hairs you have on your head. So do not be afraid. You are more important than many small birds."

MATTHEW 10:29–31

Dear God, I am amazed that You can see everything, everywhere, all the time. How do You do that? You see everything that happens. I must be really important for You to always be watching me. You want to know everything about me and everything I do. The Bible says that You even know how many hairs are on my head! Thank You for taking such good care of me, God. I'll see You in the morning. Amen.

Think about it!

In what ways does God take care of you?

God Knows My Name

"Be happy because your names are written in heaven."
LUKE 10:20

Dear God, when You look down at me from heaven, You know exactly who I am. I'm not just a kid in a crowd. I'm Yours! You know my name. Whenever You hear my name, it sounds like music to Your ears. You love saying it. The Bible says You even wrote my name in Your book in heaven. It makes me happy that You know my name. I love You, God! Amen.

Think about it!

How does it feel to know that God delights in you, His child?

I Am Alive Because of God

"It is in Him that we live and move and keep on living. Some of your own men have written, 'We are God's children.'"

Acts 17:28

Dear God, I know that everything that lives is alive because of You. All the people and all the animals on earth live because You made them. You give life to the birds in the sky, bugs that crawl, and fish in the sea. Flowers, grass, bushes, trees—everything that grows, grows because of You. You give life to everything! Thank You, God, for the gift of living. Thank You for making us all. Amen.

Think about it!

What is the most amazing animal God created and why?

God Has Planned All My Days

Your eyes saw me before I was put together. And all the days of my life were written in Your book before any of them came to be.

Psalm 139:16

Dear God, before You made me and gave me my body, You had already planned all my days. I have to wait to see what happens, but You already know. You know everything about me today, tomorrow, and always. Help me to remember that. I'm excited to find out what You have planned for me. I wonder: What will I be when I grow up? What will I look like? I can't wait to find out. Amen.

Think about it!

What do you want to be when you grow up and why?

We Are All God's Children

See what great love the Father has for us that He would call us His children. And that is what we are. For this reason the people of the world do not know who we are because they did not know Him.

1 JOHN 3:1

Dear God, it's wonderful that we are all Your children: every kid, mom, dad, grandma, grandpa, aunt, uncle, and cousin—all the people on earth are Yours. That's why we call You our heavenly Father. I'm thankful that You love us all, watch over us, and help us to be the best we can be. You know what we want, and You always give us what we need. I'm glad that I'm Your kid. Amen.

Think about it!

How does God provide for your needs?